I SHOULD
NOT BE
HERE

I SHOULD NOT BE HERE

My journey with OCD, PTSD, and depression,
and what kept me above water.

KAREN B. GERSON

KIKI Publishing

I SHOULD NOT BE HERE
My journey with OCD, PTSD, and depression,
and what kept me above water
By Karen B. Gerson

First Edition
Copyright © 2025 by Karen B. Gerson

Published by
KIKI Publishing

For permission requests,
contact MunnAvenuePress.com

Paperback ISBN: 978-1-969679-13-1
Hardcover ISBN: 978-1-969679-14-8

Printed in the United States of America

This book is not just my story.
It's a map. A mirror. A message.
You are not alone. You are not broken.
You are still here. And that means
there is still time for healing.

Karen L. Gerson

CONTENTS

MY TRUTHS
ABOUT THIS MEMOIR

THIS MEMOIR REFLECTS my personal journey with mental illness and is told through my memories and perspective. I understand that others mentioned in these pages may have experienced things differently. Still, I share my story openly, in my own voice, and without reservation. My hope is that it will resonate with those facing mental health challenges and with those who love and support them. For the sake of privacy, I've used only first names, changed some others, and, at times, chosen not to include full identifying details.

Mental illness doesn't just affect the person struggling—it ripples outward, touching everyone close. This is a resource for those living alongside someone with severe mental health challenges. I include the voices of my loved ones in this book to give representation for those who walked beside me, even when they weren't sure how. Throughout my journey, there were moments when I felt unreachable, but others were still reaching. Their reflections are honest, sometimes raw, and always rooted in love. They ask the questions you have probably wondered: *What's going to help? What can I do differently? How do I support myself while supporting them? How much of myself do I need to give? Am I helping, or is this too much for me?* If you've ever asked yourself these questions and didn't know where to turn—I wrote this book for you.

PREFACE

I SHOULDN'T BE here today. I was a meek, brown-haired, shy girl whose elementary world was consumed with carefully stepping to avoid cracks and counting every step with precision. From the moment I woke up until my eyelids closed at night, this ritual dictated my every move. If I had the misfortune of stepping on a crack or losing count, an overwhelming fear took hold that something bad was going to happen.

I shouldn't be here today. I was an uncomfortable, introverted, awkward teenager whose daily routine revolved around ensuring my closet remained in perfect order, with my clothes meticulously arranged from white to black. Afternoons were spent curled up in the back corner of that closet, creating a different life for myself, one that felt safer than the one I lived.

In high school, my emotionally fragile frame remained on high alert at all times. Whether walking alone or checking the back seat of my car as obsessive thoughts consumed me, I constantly strategized how to navigate the world without being taken, hurt, or simply seen.

I shouldn't be here today. The painfully shy and inwardly chaotic teenager who feared walking two blocks to school, whose brain was filled with constant noise, somehow graduated from high school. That should not have been possible. My second-grade teacher, Mrs. D, once told my parents, *"She is not going to amount to anything—she can't even use scissors properly."* And yet, I am here.

I shouldn't be here today. I was only accepted into college because, somehow, I must have interviewed well. I remember sitting in the admissions office at Stephens College, thinking, *How the hell did I get here?* I knew I had to nail this interview because I needed a path forward. How was I supposed to sit across from the dean, make eye contact, and answer questions like:

Why do you want to go to Stephens College?

What do you hope to accomplish here?

Where do you see yourself after graduation?

Looking someone in the eyes wasn't something I was used to. Eye contact meant vulnerability; it meant being seen. And for the past eighteen years, I had been hiding.

Fast forward to today, and I should not have:

- Transferred colleges, had a successful and loving relationship for over two years, and graduated in five years.

- Landed my first teaching job at a prestigious elementary school in the same district where I once felt invisible.

- Moved across the country, found an apartment, secured a teaching job at a private Jewish day school, built friendships, and started dating my future husband.

- Relocated to the Midwest and built an incredibly successful career in the nonprofit world—earning awards and national recognition.

- Earned my executive master's degree in Nonprofit Management.

- Stepped outside of my comfort zone and created professional opportunities beyond the Jewish community.

But behind the outward survival, I was silently battling a war within myself. My mind was a relentless storm of intrusive thoughts, an endless loop of irrational fears and rituals that I had to perform just to get through the day. I didn't want to die. However, I didn't want to live.

So, that left me no choice but to survive. The weight of undiagnosed obsessive-compulsive disorder (OCD) dictated every action, every breath, every decision. And as I grew older, it wasn't just OCD—it was the creeping darkness of post-traumatic stress disorder (PTSD) and severe depression that suffocated me, and made me question why I was the way I was, and why I couldn't simply turn off the noise, the loud background music playing twenty-four-seven in my head.

I spent years trying to unravel myself. I was desperate for answers, desperate to understand why my brain functioned this way. The fear, the rituals, the exhaustion of constantly trying to *control* an uncontrollable world—it never went away; it only evolved. And yet, through all of it, I found a way to keep going.

I shouldn't be here. And yet—

I am.

1

THE UNSEEN CHILD

Profound loneliness shaped my earliest memories. I was born into a world already filled with unmet expectations and emotional absence. My mother, Bev, was struggling with postpartum depression when she had me. Of course, I didn't understand what that meant at the time. There was a vacancy where warmth should have been, a distance that I couldn't bridge, no matter how quiet I was or how hard I tried to be good.

I now know that postpartum depression is more than just sadness. It's an overwhelming, consuming void that takes hold of a mother and makes it difficult—sometimes impossible—to connect with her child. It wasn't just that my mother was tired; she was drowning in something invisible. She was there, but she wasn't present. I think my mother wanted to be. I believe there were moments when she could lift herself from the weight of it, when she looked at me and wished she could feel the love she thought she was supposed to. But, unfortunately, during most of my childhood, that love never made it through.

My mother had given birth to my brother, Brian, only sixteen months before me. He was planned. He was expected. He was celebrated. And then, I came along. Unexpected and uninvited. My presence added to the already overwhelming stress of a life that my mother was barely managing. I imagine she must have felt trapped. Maybe she resented me for making things harder. Or maybe she just didn't have the capacity to see me at all.

I also learned that, unlike Brian, who was cradled, soothed, and given the attention of a wanted firstborn, I was not held often as a baby. My mother, still weighed down by postpartum depression, kept her distance. I imagine myself as an infant, crying out, reaching for her, only to be met with emptiness. The absence of physical affection in those early years shaped me in ways I wouldn't understand until much later. Babies need to be held and need to feel the warmth of a mother's touch to develop security in the world. I learned quickly that comfort would not come from my mother. As I struggled to understand what I might have done to cause her coldness—and how I could change to fix it—I eventually came to realize it wasn't about me.

The few moments of warmth I remember as a child didn't come from my mother. They came from others, and although fleeting, these interactions stood out because they were so rare. I fondly remember my camp counselor, Sue, who would let me sit on her lap. I remember feeling special because she had a whole camp group to look after, yet she allowed me to be close to her. It was one of the first moments where I felt chosen, where I felt like I mattered. But such moments were few and far between, and they stood in stark contrast to the pervasive void that defined my childhood.

My dad, Ed, was in his dental residency, often absent, leaving Bev alone with two babies and a suffocating sense of isolation. We lived in Dayton, Ohio, at the time. But when my dad's residency ended, my mother insisted that we move to Columbus instead of joining his family in Cleveland. It was important to her that they start their new life on their own.

We settled in Bexley, an upper-middle-class neighborhood, picturesque and orderly. My bedroom in our house was pink and green, with a green carpet like grass, and floral-patterned walls. I had a dresser with red flowers painted on it, and I remember the confusion I felt when I realized those flowers were not pink like the ones on my wall. There were two single beds in my room, but I only slept in one. I made the other bed each morning with stuffed animals placed just so—one of the first lessons in control and order that I clung to in an otherwise unpredictable world.

I started school at Cassingham Elementary, a two-story

beige brick building attached to the middle and high school. The hallways felt vast, their emptiness unsettling. I was afraid to go to the bathroom by myself. I would be alone, and to me, it was so big—more than just stalls and sinks; there were benches and even lockers, giving it an eerie locker-room feel. Walking alone through the school was uncomfortable, particularly down the long hallway to the nurse's office, where a door led directly outside to the playground. I was always afraid someone could come in unexpectedly.

Though much of my school experience was defined by anxiety, I found refuge in my kindergarten teacher, Miss Barbara. I think about her white hair and how she had a permanent warmth about her, a sense that she understood something no one else did. She greeted every child with a hug, making each of us feel chosen. I vividly remember standing with a smock at an easel, painting a flower. When Miss Barbara came over, she reacted with such enthusiasm, as if I had created a masterpiece. No one had ever expressed excitement toward me like that before. Miss Barbara had a way of making me feel seen in a world where I often felt invisible.

Another refuge was my twice-a-week tutoring with Mrs. Abby. She was thin and had kind eyes. Mrs. Abby taught me at school and at her home, a big two-story brick house with a screened porch and dogs. Her presence was comforting, even if she wasn't as outwardly affectionate as Miss

Barbara. I always received a side hug from Mrs. Abby, and there was comfort in knowing I would see her regularly. The walk to her house was only two and a half blocks, but it felt much longer. The towering trees made the streets dark, and I was always aware of my surroundings, constantly calculating an escape route in case of danger. Even as I got older, fear remained a constant companion. I checked under my bed and the back seat of my car well into adulthood, habits that only therapy helped ease.

I began counting my steps when I started elementary school and instinctively knew that wasn't typical. It was as if my mind was creating rules and systems to follow as a way to cope with something unspoken. By first grade, I already sensed that I didn't fit in. Recess was supposed to be a time for play, but while other children swung on monkey bars, played ball, or chased one another across the blacktop, I remained on the outskirts. I played by myself or, some days, just stood there, stuck. I didn't know how to initiate play, how to break into the easy camaraderie that seemed second nature to everyone else.

I did play on the swings sometimes, but I was always aware of the risks. The concrete beneath the swings seemed dangerous—I could fall, scrape my knees, or worse. If I wore a skirt, I had to be extra careful not to swing too high, or my underwear would show, and that, too, felt like a risk I wasn't willing to take. Even in moments meant for carefree childhood joy, I was calculating, cautious, always thinking ahead in ways a child shouldn't have to. I learned to exist quietly and to take up as little space as possible. Although I didn't have the language to describe the emptiness, I felt it profoundly.

Despite these small moments of kindness from teachers, my struggles in school became apparent early. By second or third grade, I was pulled into a small room with a woman who tested me for learning disabilities. My parents met with my teachers multiple times to discuss my challenges. Looking back, I think I would have thrived at a Jewish day school or private school, where the learning environment might have been more accommodating with smaller class sizes and more individual attention. Instead, I spent my school years in Bexley, where academic expectations were high, and I struggled to keep up with all the chatter and messiness that was going on in my mind.

At home, the silent battles between my parents over my place in the family left invisible scars. Tension between my parents played out in ways I wasn't meant to witness but couldn't avoid. My bedroom shared a wall with my parents' bathroom, and through that thin barrier, I overheard arguments not meant for my ears. My dad would sometimes take my side, trying to advocate for me, but his efforts were often met with my mother's fury. Eventually, he gave up, and with each surrendered argument, my sense of worth diminished further. It was as if my needs were negotiable, an inconvenience rather than a priority.

Among my siblings, I was the quiet one. Brian, the golden child, was effortlessly charming. My younger sister of five years, Malinda, was a whirlwind of rebellion, constantly demanding attention. And then there was me—compliant, nearly invisible—never the prodigy nor the problem. As a result, I learned to exist in the background, taking up as little space as possible and sought control where I could find it. I counted my steps. I arranged my belongings in precise ways. Structure became a way to cope, a way to impose order on the emotional chaos I couldn't escape. The loneliness of my early years was all-encompassing. I would sit in class, watching as other children ran toward their parents at the end of the day, receiving hugs, and being lifted effortlessly into waiting arms. I never expected to receive that myself. Instead, I walked home lost in my own head, even though Brian was next to me, counting my steps, scanning my surroundings, and bracing myself for the silence waiting for me at home.

I didn't find out I was unexpected until much later. It was a casual revelation, an offhand remark that landed like a gut punch. *"Karen, you were the oops of the family; your sister was planned,"* Bev had said one day when I was older, her tone dismissive, as if it were an insignificant detail. But it explained so much. It confirmed what I had felt my entire life—that I was an inconvenience, a complication she hadn't wanted. That moment cemented what I had always known in my gut but had never been able to put into words.

I wasn't just invisible. I was unwanted from the start. As a result, my early years were a masterclass in emotional survival. I navigated a world where my presence often went unnoticed, my achievements uncelebrated, and my pain unacknowledged. But within that darkness, the faintest sparks of resilience flickered—small, unseen, persistent reminders that deserve to be known.

OTHER
VOICES · *Shirley (Aunt Shush), My Aunt*

I am Karen's aunt. I'm the sister of her father, and I've been close to Karen, Malinda, and Brian since they were little. Of course, everyone calls me 'Aunt Shush,' and I love that.

From early on, I noticed something in Karen that felt familiar. We shared a kind of quietness, a tendency to step back from the crowd. When all the cousins gathered—nine kids under one roof during the holidays—she sometimes hung back, just like I used to. Maybe it was childhood resentment or simply our personalities, but in that, we became kindred spirits. I always felt a special bond with her.

Even during the hardest periods of her life, especially when she was hospitalized, I stayed in touch. Whenever she felt up to it, she'd come to the phone. And when she couldn't, I still remained her link to my mother—her grandmother. I never stopped being present. I was there to listen without judgment, to remind her she was loved. She called those times 'the black hole,' and I understand why, because it felt like that—like something was swallowing her up. But I never stopped believing she'd find her way out.

~~~~~~~~

THE ATTIC

The Assault

I was seven years old. It happened over Passover, the Jewish holiday celebrating the Israelites' freedom from slavery in Egypt. We were celebrating in Cleveland, where my extended family lived, a place where I felt safe. The two-story colonial house was filled with the smells of roasted chicken and matzo ball soup, the lingering voices of adults discussing things I didn't understand, and the usual chaos of family gatherings. But upstairs, beyond the reach of the warm kitchen light and the distant hum of conversation, when the kids were asleep, I was in the attic in silence. It was a forgotten space, a place of dust and old boxes, of forgotten heirlooms and the weight of things left unsaid.

That night, I felt so lucky that I got to sleep in a sleeping bag in my older cousin's room. I mean, she was in high school! Her room was pink like mine and had all her track and field medals hanging on the walls and in her bookcase. My sleeping bag was tucked, hidden between a dresser and a bed, on the far side of the room. I thought how cool it was that she was my cousin, and maybe one day I could also be like her.

I was safely asleep when a boy—who was older and stronger—was suddenly there, looming in the half-darkness. His presence was unfamiliar in a way I couldn't place. I remember the confusion first. The sudden jolt of being pulled from sleep and being dragged through a small square door to this dim attic space, with the creaking floors and the too-quiet air. I remember the way my heart pounded in my chest. I struggled to understand what was happening.

He violently took something from me that I didn't understand at the time.

I only knew that after that day, I was different.

I never told anyone. Not then. Not for years.

At seven, words didn't come to me easily, especially words for something so terrifying. I was too young to even name what had been taken from me, but my body knew. It carried the weight of that night in my muscles, in the way I flinched at sudden noises, in the way my stomach twisted when someone stood too close. My mind, though, worked quickly to bury it. It was like pushing a heavy box into the farthest corner of the attic—out of sight, out of reach—a thing I could pretend wasn't there. If I never opened that box, if I never looked inside, maybe it wouldn't be real.

But it was real. And even as I tried to forget, my body never let me.

The Aftermath

From that moment on, it consumed me entirely. My headspace was trapped in a cycle of fear and hypervigilance, making it impossible to be present. I couldn't focus on learning, on something as simple as basic math, because my biggest concern wasn't school, it was survival.

I lived in constant fear that someone was coming to get me. The older boy who assaulted me had threatened, *"If you tell anyone, I'm going to kill you."* At seven years old, I believed him. He was in high school, which in my young eyes meant he was an adult, and I had no reason to doubt his words. I wasn't old enough to feel guilt, but I was old enough to understand that speaking out meant danger.

So, I stayed silent.

As a child, I had learned that saying *no* was supposed to stop unwanted behavior. On the playground, if someone crossed a boundary, you said, *"No, please don't,"* and they listened. But I had said *no* to an adult, and he didn't stop. That was the moment I realized words wouldn't protect me. And so, I stopped talking altogether.

At home, I moved in silence, avoiding eye contact, retreating to my room immediately after school. I had

already learned that my mother had no patience for emotions. If she saw weakness, she dismissed it. If she saw tears,
she scolded. And so, I gave her nothing.

One day, the weather was beautiful, and Bev insisted
I go outside. She kept forcefully insisting that I needed to
get out of the house, but I had no idea what to do once
I was out there. We had a swing set, but being alone in
the backyard felt unsafe as no one was watching, and my
mother rarely came outside to keep an eye on me. I didn't
ride my bike by myself either; my brother was always off
at his friend's house. I remember just sitting on my bike
in the driveway, frozen, feeling paralyzed. I just sat there
until the allotted outdoor time expired by the ring of Bev's
dinner bell.

There was nowhere that felt safe.

At night, I couldn't sleep, afraid to close my eyes,
because I didn't know if someone was waiting for me. I just
couldn't be alone because I couldn't trust that I was safe. I
was consumed—utterly consumed—by fear.

My dad, Ed, would sometimes glance at me with concern, as if he knew something was off but didn't have the
tools—or the courage—to ask. But as always, he deferred
to Bev, who saw my withdrawal as nothing more than me
being difficult. In our house, there was no room for the messy
emotions of a child who had been hurt.

As a result, the weight of that night lived inside my small
body, manifesting in ways I couldn't control. I couldn't walk

the halls alone at school, so I held my bladder until I couldn't anymore, forcing myself to use the school's bathrooms even though they felt unsafe. I also memorized hiding spots on my way to school, places I could duck into if someone tried to grab me. I held my breath past unfamiliar cars, convinced that looking too long might make me visible. I tracked which houses had dogs, which had windows low enough to knock on in an emergency. My world became a constant state of survival.

While my kid brain couldn't make sense of what had happened to me, I still could make sure the things in my world stayed exactly as they should be. This is when my compulsion for control, already present, amplified and became all-encompassing. I counted my steps, making sure I reached my room in the same number each time. I reorganized my belongings obsessively, making sure my collection of glass animals aligned perfectly; my clothes were folded just right. If something was out of place, panic would rise in my chest like a tidal wave. I couldn't control what had happened in that attic, but I could control my immediate surroundings. My OCD was now on steroids. All the while, I had stopped reading aloud in school and strug-gled to complete assignments. I felt as if I was there, but I wasn't really there.

This was the start of therapy. Family therapy. Individual therapy. None of it helped. I refused to speak, refused to open the door to what was buried inside me. I was afraid for my life. The therapists weren't prepared for a child like me—a child who had been silenced in more ways than one. They asked me about school, about my interests. They asked what I wanted to talk about. I didn't want to talk about anything. I didn't know how to. But no one ever asked, *"Has anyone hurt you?"* or *"Do you feel safe at home?"* Nothing. So, the sessions were just another thing I endured.

Each day at dusk, I rearranged my room in complete silence, waiting for my dad to come home. Sitting on my bed, I would first hear, then watch the garage door open from the window of my room and know he was home. There were moments I felt a sense of ease in his presence, when he would sit with me, drill me on schoolwork, and it seemed— just for a little while—that I mattered. But he never asked about the shadows under my eyes or the way I flinched at loud noises. Maybe Ed didn't want to know.

Eventually, my room, and specifically the closet, became my refuge. I would disappear into its small, dark space, close the door behind me, and press my back against its cool wall. Inside, I was safe. Inside, the outside world couldn't touch me. I would arrange my shoes in a precise order, straighten the hangers, and refold clothes over and over again, until they were perfect. I whispered numbers to myself, making sure I reached the right total. I created patterns, rituals— things that made sense when nothing else did.

I then developed more rituals beyond the closet. In addition to avoiding cracks on sidewalks, I held my breath while walking past doorways and traced the edges of my school desk with my fingers, always in the same pattern. These compulsions were my armor, my way of keeping the unknown at bay. If I did things in the right order, if I followed my own set of invisible rules, then maybe I could keep bad things from happening again.

My parents had close friends about ten minutes away by car, the Brooksteins. They would come over occasionally, but we visited their house far more often than they came to ours. I always wondered why that was, but I loved any chance to leave my house and go there. Their daughter, Lily, was my age, and she had a really cool closet. Still, I never liked being in it, even when my brother, Lily, and I would hang out there together. It wasn't *my* closet, and something about it made me uncomfortable. I also never liked being alone with her dad, even though he was my dad's close friend. He never did anything inappropriate, but I felt uneasy being alone with any adult man. Despite that, I still enjoyed being at their house; it felt different, like an escape.

Much later in life, I would understand why I avoided intimacy, why I had an aversion to attics, and being alone with men aside from my brother and dad. I never had the words, not even in college. When driving past the house where it happened years later, I finally whispered to a friend, *"I think someone hurt me here."* I didn't say, *"I was sexually assaulted."* I didn't say, *"I was raped."* I only knew something wrong had happened there.

It wasn't until my forties that I sought treatment at a facility called Onsite in Tennessee, an inpatient facility specializing in PTSD, that I fully confronted the truth. Through EMDR therapy, I realized my mind had been peeling back layers, revealing what I had buried. EMDR, by the way, stands for eye movement desensitization and reprocessing, and is a psychotherapy designed to help people process traumatic memories and alleviate distress associated with them. It involves recalling traumatic events while engaging in bilateral stimulation, such as side-to-side eye movements, to facilitate healing and reduce symptoms of conditions like PTSD.

Healing didn't come easily, and it isn't a linear path. But at Onsite, I learned that my silence hadn't protected me—it had only prolonged my suffering. The real work began when I allowed myself to remember. It was terrifying, but for the first time, I wasn't alone.

I remember my EMDR specialist explaining that the emotional brain is like an onion—you can only peel back one layer at a time. It doesn't open all at once. Each layer reveals itself only when your body is ready to process it. I've always liked that analogy because it's so tangible, as most people can easily picture the layers of an onion and how they're revealed gradually. The same was true for me: My process of healing mirrored the onion analogy. I would remember things as they presented themselves, when my body allowed the memories, one layer at a time. I later learned this was a normal reaction to trauma. Details would slowly uncover themselves over time. I find it amazing how the brain only gives you what you can handle and protects the rest. In turn, there would be no quick fix.

I never wanted to confront my attacker. I knew, deep down, that people in my family probably had an unspoken understanding of what had happened. He was an outcast, distant from everyone, struggling with severe health issues, and had been disconnected from the family for years. But after I came back from Onsite, I had a conversation with a family member. She kept pressing me over and over— *"Who did it? Who did it?"*—like she already knew but needed me to say it. She was relentless. I didn't want to tell her, but eventually, I just blurted it out. Her response, *"Oh, that makes sense,"* was almost casual, as if she had been expecting it. Then she told me about another sexual assault by another family member that happened within the family years before.

In that moment, it was clear: This wasn't just something that happened to me. This had happened before in our family. But even after knowing all this, I never had any desire to confront my attacker. When talk of family reunions came up, I made my stance clear—if he was going to be there, I wasn't. THAT family member seemed surprised when I refused, but I think, deep down, she already knew why. His isolation from the family wasn't a coincidence. It wasn't some mystery. But, in my family, things like this were never openly discussed.

Silence was just the way things were handled.

I wish someone had asked the right question when I was a child.

Maybe then, I wouldn't have spent decades locked inside my own silence.

OTHER
VOICES   *Eitan, My Son*

I'm Eitan, my mom's youngest son. I'm fifteen now, but the first time I realized something serious was going on with my mom, I was probably in third or fourth grade. I don't remember the exact moment—it just kind of crept in. She was in bed a lot, more than usual. And she wasn't really around like she used to be. I'd get up and maybe she'd take me to school, but that didn't happen often. I'd come home and sort of figure out my day on my own. Sometimes my dad was around, sometimes not, depending on work. But mostly, she was in bed. And I really didn't have much help with stuff.

At the time, I didn't fully understand what was happening. I'd check in on her, ask if she needed water or anything. But I didn't get that it was mental illness. I didn't know what depression was. I just knew my mom wasn't there in the way she had been before, and that was really hard.

It wasn't until a few years later, after I started going to therapy and talking to people about it, that I began to understand. I realized that what my mom was going through wasn't the kind of illness where you're going to die, but something deeper—mental illness. I still struggle with anxiety myself, and I think part of it came from that time. But having the words to explain it made a difference.

3

~~~~~

GROUNDHOG DAY

I BURIED MY assault deep, pressing it down into the farthest corners of my mind, locking it away where even I couldn't reach it. Out of sight. Out of thought. Out of existence.

Or at least, that's what I told myself.

But even though I forced it down, its weight never left me. It lived in the way I moved through the world—cautious, small, invisible. By the time I entered middle school, I had mastered the art of disappearing. I wasn't the child who raised her hand in class or called out the answers. I wasn't the one playing or joining in the chaos of the lunchroom. I wasn't the girl who spoke too loudly or took up too much space. Instead, I hovered at the edges, careful, quiet, unnoticed. It was safer that way. If no one saw me, no one could hurt me.

A Typical Morning

Every day felt like Groundhog Day. I would close my eyes at night, hoping that something would magically change when I woke. However, morning would come, and everything would be exactly the same.

A typical morning of getting ready for school followed the same pattern—if I was lucky. I had to get up on the same side of the bed, or my OCD determined it would be a bad day. Then came the shower: get my entire body wet first, then shampoo my hair. While the shampoo was still in, I would clean the left side of my body, then rinse both the shampoo and the left side. Next, conditioner for my hair while washing the right side of my body. Once the water was off, it was time to towel dry, always in the same order— right arm, then left, stomach area, back, right leg, left leg, and finally, wrapping the towel around my body.

Not sure if you had to squeegee your shower at a young age, but in my household, streaks and dry spots were not allowed. Bev had to have the entire house just so. And, of course, there was a ritual to this process as well. Are you exhausted yet? I haven't even gotten dressed, had breakfast, or left for school.

I don't think I chose my clothing in a certain way. But I do remember stepping into my closet (where, of course, everything was arranged in color order), and despite having plenty of options, never being particularly excited about them. That's because I knew that no matter what I wore on the outside, I would still be the same person on the inside. But there was one exception: a pair of knickers that Bev bought me. I loved them because they were in style, and for once, I had something fashionable. And I never liked the way jeans fit; they felt like they were hugging my private parts, which looked and felt awkward. I also didn't like looking at myself in the mirror. The irony was that my room had a full-length mirror and another above my chest of drawers, making it nearly impossible to avoid my reflection.

In the hallway on the way downstairs, I had to check the dictionary on top of a wooden cart to ensure it was open and verify that the full set of burgundy encyclopedias was in alphabetical order and accounted for. *Phew*. Now the stairs. The carpet on the stairs was dark blue in my early years (mauve in middle and high school). The steps had to be counted, for *"everything to be okay."* I didn't know what that meant, only that if I didn't count, my brain warned me that things would not be good. Just making it down the stairs felt like a chore.

My dad would sit at the breakfast table, reading the newspaper and shaving at the same time. He didn't engage much during breakfast—unless he was quizzing me for a test, which I absolutely hated. Breakfast was always unsweetened cereal since Ed was an endodontist, and nothing with overt sugar, including soda, was allowed in our house. The choices were Cheerios, Rice Krispies, and Raisin

Bran. Rice Krispies got soggy too quickly, and Raisin Bran, well, had raisins—which I didn't like at the time (though in hindsight, I probably should have appreciated the sugar coating on them). I'd have orange juice, but never the pre-made kind. Instead, we'd buy the frozen concentrate in a can and mix it with water.

I don't remember much about making my lunch. But I do recall the sinking feeling that came with lunchtime, knowing I'd be sitting by myself. Then came the two-block walk to school, on which most days Brian and I walked together. On the rare days that Brian went in early for viola or Safety Patrol, these were my inner thoughts:

Two doors down, I had to pass the "X" house—the house with a gun inside. I always worried: What if he came out and shot me?

Then came the crosswalk—I had to make it while the sign still said "WALK." *Hurry! Run!*

Then block number two. Far enough from home that I couldn't run back, and too far from school to feel safe. The islands in between the sides of the streets were lined with trees—beautiful to most, but to me, they were the best places to hide if someone followed me by car and tried to kidnap me.

This is the way my brain worked.

School should have been a refuge, but it wasn't. The other kids had an ease about them that I envied. They laughed without hesitation, played games without fear. I, on the other hand, found solace in structure and solitude. I dreaded reading aloud in class, terrified of stumbling over words, of drawing attention to myself.

School wasn't just a place of isolation—it was a place of quiet dread—a minefield of situations I tried to avoid. When the teacher called on students to answer questions, I would hold my breath, willing myself to disappear. But it was inevitable that I would be called on. In second grade, I remember the moment my teacher called my name and asked me to come up to the board to solve a math problem. My stomach dropped. I hadn't been following the lesson. Numbers had always felt like a foreign language, something everyone else seemed to understand while I just pretended to keep up.

As I stood there with chalk in my trembling fingers, my mind went completely blank. The problem on the board swam before me, and I couldn't even bring myself to guess. The silence in the room stretched, and I could feel my classmates shifting in their seats, waiting, watching. My chest tightened, my ears burned, and I became hyper aware of every tiny movement—someone tapping their pencil, a chair creaking, the sound of my breathing getting faster. I knew I couldn't stand there forever, but I couldn't force my mouth to form the words: *I don't know*, as saying it out loud would make it real. Instead, I stared at the board, willing the answer to come, wishing the floor would swallow me whole.

It wasn't just during math class—I felt this way all the time. Even in the library, when we were given free time to pick out books, something that should have felt easy, I froze. The shelves stretched endlessly before me, with too many options, too many decisions I didn't trust myself to make. The other kids browsed with ease, pulling books off the shelves without hesitation, flipping through the pages, and finding something that excited them. I envied how effortless it was for them. Meanwhile, I stood there, unable to move, my fingers hovering over the spines of books I'd never pick up. If I made the wrong choice, would the librarian notice? Would my teacher judge me? Would I prove, yet again, that I didn't belong? It felt like everyone else had been handed a guidebook on how to navigate the world, and I was the only one left wandering without a map.

As I got older, my isolation became more profound. In middle school, my classmates became more social, forming friendships that carried them through the awkwardness of adolescence. I remained stuck, though, unable to cross the invisible barrier between myself and others. I observed their interactions, studying them as if understanding their ease would somehow allow me to replicate it.

The only moments I felt any relief were when I was alone in my structured world. I found solace in the repetition of my routines. I counted my steps, tapped the corners of my desk a certain number of times, and recited silent prayers before stepping into rooms. These rituals became my anchor, a way to ground myself in a reality that otherwise felt unpredictable and unsafe. And so, I continued in my isolation, learning to exist in the spaces between, in the silence, in the places where no one was looking.

And in that silence, I began to disappear into myself, my rituals, and the quiet certainty that I was alone.

Coming Back from School: The Silent Rules of Home

Dinner in our house wasn't a time for connection—it was another routine, another silent performance where each of us played our expected role. We had assigned seats at the table, just like we had assigned chores: setting the table, clearing the dishes, and unloading the dishwasher. I remember carefully placing each fork to the left, the spoon and knife to the right, ensuring that even the napkin was folded just so because that's how it had to be. My mother rarely spoke unless it was to criticize something small, like the way my sister chewed with her mouth open. I remember her saying how disgusting it was and threatening to bring a mirror to the table so my sister could watch herself. Even as a child, I knew how cruel that was. I wanted to say something to defend my sister, but I knew better. Saying the wrong thing could shift the mood, and I had learned early that staying quiet was safer.

Conversations at the table were surface-level at best, obligatory at worst. My dad would ask the usual, *"How was your day?"* and I would answer with a default, *"Fine."* What else could I say? That I had spent lunch sitting alone? That I had been terrified all day about being called on in class? That even picking out a book in the library felt impossible? No. So, I kept it simple, offering just enough of a response to move the conversation forward without inviting more questions. The only real interaction was about the food—*Pass the chicken, More cinnamon and sugar for my noodles*—functional requests that filled the silence but never the emptiness.

Even the meals themselves were dictated by unspoken rules. Dessert wasn't a nightly thing, but on rare occasions, my mother would bake chocolate chip oatmeal cookies on a Friday afternoon. I loved sneaking bits of raw cookie dough. It was one of the few small joys I could grasp onto in a house that otherwise felt cold.

Most nights, when dinner was over, I would retreat upstairs to my room—my safe space, my controlled world—where I didn't have to worry about saying the wrong thing or making the wrong move. Where silence wasn't uncomfortable—it was just mine.

Finding Safety at Camp

If there was one place where I could breathe, it was overnight summer camp. But it wasn't immediate. Camp Ramah, nestled in the Northwoods of Conover, Wisconsin, is a vibrant overnight Jewish camp that brings together kids from across the Midwest. More than just a summer escape, it's a place where Jewish identity is woven into every aspect of camp life. Whether we were learning Hebrew, sailing across the lake, competing in sports, or gathering around a crackling campfire, Judaism was seamlessly infused into the experience. It wasn't just a camp—it was a world where tradition, community, and adventure came together under the open sky.

Even so, at first, camp felt foreign. I was used to isolation, and suddenly, I was surrounded by other kids who seemed to flow naturally in and out of conversations, friendships forming effortlessly. I was an outsider here too—at least at first. Hebrew school had never been my strength, and Ramah was steeped in the culture and language I struggled with. The other kids spoke Hebrew fluently, knew the songs, the prayers, and I didn't.

Every summer, we put on a camp play entirely in Hebrew. It was a big deal, and all the kids and staff looked forward to the production. I remember trying out for the camp play each year and feeling like I didn't belong. The script was in Hebrew, and while others recited their lines with confidence, I stumbled. I stayed in the background, hesitant, not knowing how to step forward. It wasn't until my final year at camp that I dared to audition properly. And to my shock, I landed a major role. It was the first time I felt I had earned a place.

And camp was also the first place where I felt the warmth of connection. My counselors—women who showed kindness I wasn't used to—took an interest in me. At first, I was suspicious. Why were they nice? What did they want? But over time, I started to trust that maybe, just maybe, they cared.

Camp was also where I first began to think about and ask questions regarding Judaism and how it related to me in my life. I remember coming home one summer and asking my mother if we could keep kosher or follow Jewish dietary laws. It made no sense to me that at camp, we followed the rules, but at home, we didn't. My mother's response? She pulled open a kitchen drawer and said, *"You can keep your kosher things in here."* End of discussion. It was always like that—no conversation, no curiosity, just dismissal.

Even though camp had been overwhelming at first, it slowly became one of the few places where I could breathe. It wasn't easy, as I still felt like an outsider in so many ways. But there was something different about being there. The structure, the rituals, the way Shabbat or the Jewish Sabbath felt special, even the way the lake shimmered in the late afternoon light—it all made me feel like I was part of something, even if I wasn't sure what that something was yet. As my Jewish identity was forming at camp, I began to wonder where I fit in. At home, Judaism felt more like a set of rules to follow, things we did because we were supposed to. But at camp, it felt alive. It was in the songs we sang, the prayers whispered before bed, the way the counselors talked about traditions like they meant something. I wasn't sure what any of it meant to me yet, but I knew it felt different from how it did at home.

The best part was that no one at camp knew me from back home. I wasn't the girl who sat alone at lunch or the one who barely spoke in class. I wasn't weighed down by the expectations of my family, the rules of my house, or the invisible label I carried in school. I wish I could have found a way to bring Camp Me back home, but that wasn't a reality. Home meant the disapproving looks from Bev, isolating me, and making me feel small. At camp, I could be whoever I wanted to be or at least try. I could talk more if I wanted. I could let myself laugh without second-guessing. I could join in without overthinking whether I belonged. No one had already decided who I was, so for the first time, I got to decide for myself. Because at camp, there were no disapproving looks. Despite the struggles I had—feeling lost in Hebrew, worrying if I was getting things right, still carrying pieces of my isolation with me—camp was one of the only places where I wasn't invisible.

Even when I didn't fully belong, I was still seen.

OTHER VOICES   *Elisa, My Longtime Friend*

I have known Karen—whom I lovingly call 'Bonehead'—since we first met in 1984 during our summers at Camp Ramah in Conover, Wisconsin. She calls me Bonehead, too. We were bunkmates. From the beginning, Karen was kind, vibrant, effortlessly put together, and magnetic—everyone loved her. She arrived each summer with a fresh, stylish haircut and an air of quiet confidence. I've always adored her deep, sultry voice; it still makes me smile.

When I first learned that Bonehead was struggling with her mental health, I reached out immediately. She's my dear friend, but it was also deeply personal as I had my own hidden history with mental illness. My mother was both mentally and physically ill for most of my life, and camp had been my sanctuary, too. It was where I felt the most me.

I never talked about it back then, but I can now: I carried shame, sadness, and embarrassment about my upbringing. My brother also lives with mental illness. So, I understood on some level and knew I wanted to show up for Bonehead in a way that said, "You are not alone."

Even when we weren't in constant contact, I stayed present through texts and voice messages—telling her that I loved her, that I was here, that she didn't need to respond. I tried to be a steady presence.

When Bonehead was doing well, our friendship picked up just as it had when we were twelve and thirteen, like no time had passed. But there were definitely times when we were more in touch than others. I wish I had been more present during certain stretches, especially when I didn't fully understand what was going on. I knew she was depressed, but not the full scope until more recently. Even then, I never questioned staying connected—I just tried to keep reaching out with love and patience.

Our friendship has only deepened. Karen has also been an incredible support to me, especially when I needed guidance for helping others close to me who live with mental illness. The more I learn about her journey, the more in awe I am. I try to tell her that as often as I can.

Karen—Bonehead—is one of the strongest people I've ever known. She's also one of the most fiercely loyal. She would do anything for the people she truly loves.

4

JUST MAKE IT TO GRADUATION

BY THE TIME I reached high school, I had perfected the art of being unnoticed. I had spent years mastering how to exist without drawing attention and how to navigate the world without disrupting it. But something inside of me was shifting. The quiet, invisible girl I had always been was starting to sense a desperation for control over my life, my body, and my place in the world.

High school was a place where everything seemed to have its own social order, and I, as always, felt like an outsider. I watched as friendships formed effortlessly, as groups clustered in hallways, as classmates planned their weekends with an ease I could never muster. I didn't know how to insert myself into the rhythm of their lives because I never quite belonged anywhere; I was always on the periphery. Although I was technically present for my life, it was as if I were watching a slow-motion movie from the outside.

Bexley High School:
A Pressure Cooker of Expectations

Bexley High School is a small, highly competitive public school, often compared to elite private institutions in its academic rigor. My graduating class consisted of 136 students, and nearly everyone was expected to attend college, with an exceptionally high percentage of graduates attending top universities. The school was well-funded, its faculty experienced, and its students driven. For many, success was measured in GPA, ACT, and SAT scores, college acceptance letters, and extracurricular achievements. In this environment, mediocrity was not an option.

For me, school was a minefield. Despite my perception of struggling academically, my final GPA was above a 3.0—solidly above average in such a high-performing school. However, a distinct pattern emerged in my grades, one I didn't recognize at the time: Every year, during the third quarter—right around Passover, the anniversary of the time when the assault had happened—my grades would plummet.

My usual A's and B's would drop into the C range, sometimes lower. It was as if my body knew before my mind did, as if the trauma was imprinted in my calendar. The weight of that season would press down on me, dulling my ability to concentrate, draining my energy. By the fourth quarter, my grades would recover as the season shifted, and I would push forward, functioning without ever truly processing. No teacher asked why this pattern existed. They saw me as a "nice young lady," a polite student, someone who wasn't a problem. And I made sure to keep it that way.

OCD & High School Routines

The routines that had structured my childhood—counting steps, obsessive showering, organizing objects for a sense of control—continued into high school, but the stakes felt higher. I had to walk the same way every day, step on the same cracks, and ensure I followed the same invisible rules to maintain the fragile order in my life.

Walking to and from school was another battle. If I had to walk alone in the dark—after a football game, after band practice—it became a desperate exercise in survival. I knew exactly where every streetlight was, crossing the road strategically to stay in the glow of whatever dim protection they offered. The fear of being alone, of something happening, of simply existing in the open, was constant. Yet I told no one.

I joined the marching band because I needed an art credit for my graduation requirements. I was not able to draw or paint, theater was another version of being called to the chalkboard, and I had no singing voice so through the process of elimination, band was it. Unfortunately, it became another source of anxiety. Playing the flute while marching was too much for me—I couldn't focus on both at the same time. My teacher must have known I wasn't good, but he still gave me an A-minus, probably out of kindness. I spent more time worrying about how I'd get home after late-night games than I did about the actual music, as my parents would tell me it was too late to pick me up. I never went out afterward. Everyone else would head to Friendly's for ice cream or someone's house, but I would make my way home, repeating to myself, *"Just get home safe."* Those two and a half blocks felt like miles.

Friendships: Searching for Warmth

Friendships in high school were complicated. I had people I sat next to and partnered with for assignments, but few I would call close.

Ginni had been a friend since elementary school, and I went to her house a few times. I loved it there. Her mother greeted us at the door, offered snacks, and made me feel welcome in a way I rarely felt at home.

Then there was Nellie. My mother didn't like her, which meant I never invited her over, but I spent plenty of time at her house. Her mother wasn't warm, but she also wasn't harsh, and that was enough for me. We spent time together, but our friendship had its limits—we never slept over at each other's houses or crossed certain lines of closeness.

There were moments in high school where I felt completely lost. I remember once in biology class, while dissecting a frog with Ginni, my lab partner, who was destined for medical school—how she handled everything while I sat there, staring at the formaldehyde-soaked body in front of me, unable to process how she matched its insides to the textbook diagram. I relied on her to get through the assignment. I was grateful, but I also felt like an outsider even in that small, two-person setting.

Ramah Israel: A Shift in Perspective

The Ramah Israel trip, an extension of Camp Ramah held in Israel at the end of my junior year of high school, was a pivotal experience. And not just because it was my first extended time away from home abroad, but because it was one of the first times I recognized my own power over my mindset.

Unlike Camp Ramah in Wisconsin, where Jewish life was seamlessly blended with sailing, sports, and campfires, the Israel abroad program was physically and emotionally challenging. Camp had always felt like a second home—a place filled with familiar faces from across the Midwest, where I learned Hebrew, celebrated Shabbat under the stars, and spent my days swimming and playing games by the lake. Camp in Israel was different. It was an adventure, but it also demanded more from me.

From the very first day, I was pushed beyond my comfort zone. We arrived in Israel in mid-June, and the heat was oppressive. But there was no time to settle in or adjust.

Straight from the airport, we were sent on a grueling hike up a mountain. The exhaustion set in immediately. I was jet-lagged, sweating profusely, dehydrated, and miserable. My internal dialogue was relentless: *This sucks. Why are we doing this?* I could hear my negativity, a steady loop of complaints that only made things feel worse. I knew my friends were chatting and laughing, excited to be there, but I was too caught up in my frustration to join in.

Then, somewhere along the climb, something shifted. It wasn't a grand revelation, just a simple realization: I had a choice. I could spend the next six weeks miserable, complaining, and resenting every difficult moment, or I could accept where I was and try to make the best of it. For the first time, I recognized that I wasn't stuck in my head—I could actually change the way I experienced things. I let go of the frustration, took a deep breath, and tried to be present.

This moment felt significant because I had never thought that way before. My default had always been to brace for the worst, to assume discomfort, and to dwell in negativity. But in Israel, far from my family and the familiar patterns of home, I felt a sense of independence I hadn't known before. In Israel, I wasn't told what to do, what to wear, or how to act. I was in charge of myself. I was responsible for my own experience.

That realization stayed with me throughout the trip. However, I wasn't suddenly a different person. There were still moments of frustration, still times I wished for the ease of camp in Wisconsin, but I had learned something about perspective and control. It was a small shift, but it was the first time I saw a version of myself that didn't feel powerless.

Finding Work, Finding a Mother

When I returned home, I looked for any excuse to be out of my house. I also needed to make money if I wanted to do anything social, go to the movies, or pay for gas. So, I always worked. I took babysitting jobs, worked at a pharmacy, and later at a jewelry store. But it was at Madison's, a women's clothing store, where something deeper began to take shape. At Madison's, I was needed. When the holiday season came, I was the one who wrapped gifts—something no one else wanted to do. The older women customers would sigh with relief when they saw me, saying, *"Oh, thank God you're here, Karen."* They appreciated me, praised me, and relied on me. In those moments, I felt like I mattered. I became the reliable, responsible girl they could count on, the eager helper who found joy in simple acts of service.

I also excelled at organizing the store, making sure the hangers faced the same way, that the clothing racks were perfectly spaced, and that everything looked exactly as it should. My OCD, which controlled so many aspects of my life, found an outlet in the precision of retail. The other employees saw me as diligent and hardworking, but for me, it was more than that; it was about creating order in a world that felt chaotic.

Only later would I realize that it wasn't just about the work. Without knowing it, I was seeking something I had never received at home: a mother's approval. The older women, both customers and the staff at the store, with their casual warmth, their small compliments, their reliance on me, unknowingly filled a space that had been empty for so long. At Madison's, I wasn't just an employee, I was someone's daughter, if only for a few hours at a time.

This longing for a maternal connection extended beyond work. It showed up in the way I gravitated toward friends' mothers who were warm and welcoming. This longing was also there with my teachers, particularly Mrs. Kraus, my English and speech teacher, who offered me stability in an environment where I otherwise felt adrift. She and her husband, Jack, hired me as their regular babysitter, and every Saturday night, I spent time in their home. Unlike my own house, where I often felt like an afterthought, their home was structured and predictable. I knew what to expect—an evening with the kids, twenty dollars in my pocket at the end, and a feeling, however brief, that I belonged somewhere. Overall, looking back, I was subconsciously creating a mother-daughter dynamic with the older women who were in my life. But even with the sense of purpose I found at work, a deep depression set in as I realized that Camp Ramah—my lifelong refuge—was ending, and now my last escape was slipping away, too.

BBYO: Losing My Safe Place

I joined the B'nai B'rith Youth Organization (BBYO), a Jewish youth group, in high school. People didn't know me, except as the sister of my popular brother. It gave me the chance to get away. I learned to mask and appreciate the time away from my house. My brother established the relationships, and I was along for the ride. I was lucky that he was successful in this, and he spoke for me. As a result, I was no longer afraid of being made fun of, and I was with other Jewish teens, all which felt comfortable. Overall, people were kind. I also chose a chapter that had upperclasswomen in it. They loved having a freshman member. I remember going to the first event for my chapter and feeling very welcome. For the first time, I didn't need to prove myself, and the girls wanted to take care of and mentor me. It was this mentoring that helped me become a leader in the organization later on.

So, BBYO and Ramah had been my escapes, my refuges from the rest of my life. Places where I wasn't invisible, where I could be the version of myself that I wanted to be. I had leadership roles, I had a purpose, and for once, I felt seen. But as senior year wound down, I could feel all of this slipping away. The final BBYO convention was meant to be a sendoff, a celebration. But for me, it was something else. It was an ending.

I had built my identity within BBYO, and now it was disappearing. Without it, all I had left was school. This realization set in slowly, and with it came a crushing sense of loss. The countdown had begun—not to something exciting, but to the end of the school year, the last marker of structure before I was left with nothing. I kept telling myself, "Just make it to graduation." But the anxiety was growing, and depression set in. I lost weight unknowingly. Now, with BBYO ending, the last piece of my safe space was gone, and I began slipping further into myself.

A Hollow Victory

By the end of the school year, I had shrunk from a size eight to a size two. At graduation, I stood in a white dress with gold detailing, physically the smallest I had ever been, and emotionally felt like I was vanishing. As I looked around at my classmates, celebrating and planning for their futures, I realized that I had no idea what came next.

I had spent years structuring my life around distractions—BBYO, jobs, rituals, and survival. I had no more track to guide my life, no more living toward summer escapes at Ramah or counting down days to a BBYO convention. Now, as I faced the next chapter, I was left with nothing but myself and a feeling of complete emptiness and despair. And that terrified me.

OTHER
VOICES   *Harriette, My Teacher and Friend*

I first met Karen when she was a freshman in high school. I was her speech teacher that year, and I had a one-year-old at home. We were in the middle of moving to a new place, and I asked Karen if she babysat. She said yes. That very same day—our chaotic moving day—I brought her over, and she ended up having to take my baby to my parents' house, put him to bed, and handle the whole evening. She did it all with such ease and maturity. After that, she became our regular babysitter every weekend. Over time, we grew very close.

Karen had a strong group of friends in high school through BBYO and camp. She seemed steady, grounded, and joyful during that period. I didn't realize the extent of her difficulties at home until much later. Her mom always struck me as very strict and someone hard to communicate with. But Karen never showed any signs that something was seriously wrong, not in high school. She was always warm, responsible, and fun to be around. Our house was full of laughter when she and her friends came over.

It wasn't until college that I began to notice shifts. She went away to Stephens College, and I'm still not exactly sure what happened there, as she didn't talk much about it. Later, she was at Ohio State, and I learned that her parents wouldn't let her come back home. That's when I told her she could stay with us as we had a spare bedroom, and my husband was setting up a business out of town.

It seemed like a good situation, and I trusted her completely. Even then, though, I didn't recognize the deeper struggles she was facing.

There were hints. She would say things like, "I'm not sure about my sexuality," or "I feel uncertain about who I am." But I was juggling young kids, teaching, and a big move—it was easy to chalk it up to typical college uncertainty. She was so good at keeping up a brave front, at seeming fine.

Looking back, I realize she never really confided in me until years later. I think she wanted to preserve a certain image—maybe because I'd been her teacher, maybe because I always told her how much I admired her life and her friendships. I truly did. I used to say, "I hope my kids grow up to have what you have." But I see now that there was a lot I didn't understand.

What I wish people knew about Karen is how much is always swirling in her mind. When she talks a lot, it's not because she's scattered or overcommunicating—it's because she needs to talk it through to make sense of what's going on inside. She is incredibly kind and would do anything for someone she loves, but there are roadblocks inside her that make it hard for that generosity to always come through. Getting the right treatment has helped her so much—those blockages have lessened, and the caring, grounded Karen has reemerged more fully.

5

~~~~~~

COLLEGE AND
CRUMBLING ILLUSIONS

I WASN'T READY for college, but I went anyway. It had nothing to do with intelligence or work ethic. I was capable—on paper, I made sense. But internally, I was still a child trying to play the role of an adult. I lacked a sense of self, of stability. Of safety. I had spent so long blending in, surviving without being noticed, that the thought of stepping into a new place, full of strangers and expectations, felt terrifying.

My choice of Stephens College wasn't really a choice. It was a logical suggestion because my cousin went there, and acceptance was based on my experience rather than test scores. Stephens was a small women's college in Columbia, Missouri. My best friend from high school, Nellie, was going, too. It seemed like I'd have a few footholds. But from the moment my parents dropped me off and drove away—earlier than expected, without ceremony—I was unmoored.

There were no traditions to fall back on. No rhythm. Just the unfamiliar.

My dorm room had hardwood floors and a strange stillness. I remember unpacking, not really decorating, and sitting on my bed as silence filled the space. Nellie and my cousin were on another floor. They became close quickly, while I became a ghost.

Stephens was beautiful—brick buildings, old trees, sunlight filtering through windows in serene classrooms. But I felt miles away from myself. I tried to build a routine. I found solace in one hour of television each day. *Days of Our Lives* became my anchor. I would rush back from lunch, sink into the common room couch, and disappear into the lives of fictional people who felt more vivid than I did. It reminded me of hiding in my closet as a child. I could vanish into another world, one where I didn't have to be me. For that hour, I didn't have to explain anything to anyone. It was control through detachment. Survival through story.

I did try to engage. I volunteered to teach Sunday school at the local synagogue. I found Ava, a Jewish student from Seattle who felt like a lifeline. We shared a cultural shorthand—a comfort in familiar rituals, foods, and holidays. We weren't best friends, but we understood each other. Unfortunately, due to a dire family circumstance, she left after the first semester. I recall feeling guilty about feeling bad for myself because I had just lost a friend, rather than empathetic for my friend. The situation was confusing for me. I wanted to be a good person and be supportive of her. But I was sad about her leaving me. We would study together, and on the weekend, we'd watch movies and eat meals together. I was losing one of my only friends, and friends to me were a rare commodity. I didn't know how to navigate these conflicting feelings and judged myself harshly.

I attended Shabbat dinners with a professor who regularly invited students into her home. That hour around the table with the flicker of candles, the warmth of challah, and the familiar blessings was like oxygen. I was also lucky that Stephens College was near the University of Missouri, where other Ramahniks went. One of them was Lisa, who was a few years older than me and whom I knew from camp. We shared an easy connection. For Rosh Hashanah, the Jewish new year, she invited me to her family's home in St. Louis. I remember watching them move through their rituals with such ease and grace, and for the first time in a long time, I felt like I genuinely belonged.

But there was a pattern: brief moments of connection followed by withdrawal. People left, or they had no room for me. Nellie and my cousin drifted away, folding into each other. My new roommate Jenny spent most weekends with her boyfriend in St. Louis. When she was around, I was ecstatic. At least there was another presence in the room. But mostly, I was alone. She also left after the first semester.

However, I did what I was supposed to do. I showed up. I joined Jewish Life on campus. I even dated. But the thread running through all of these activities was detachment. Like I was playing the part of a college student, but had no idea what the story was about.

The closest I felt to being seen came through small gestures—my dad sending me holiday baskets for Passover or Rosh Hashanah, each one carefully timed and deeply symbolic. It meant he saw me. Or at least tried to. But there was still a gap for me.

Then came the pivot: my mother's proposal. If I transferred to Ohio State, the family would take a vacation together. An emotional trade for a vacation—but it landed. I hadn't built anything lasting at Stephens. I was adrift, disconnected. The promise of being part of something, even a trip, felt like a tether. So, I said *yes*. I packed up, sent my things home, and enrolled at Ohio State.

And that's where I met Alex.

He was my brother's girlfriend's best friend from high school. A completely random connection. But he became my everything. With Alex, I experienced warmth. Presence. Humor. We built a bubble around ourselves—a small, strange, wonderful cocoon. He waited for me after class. He walked with me across the massive Ohio State campus. He made me laugh in a way that cracked open something frozen inside me. I learned joy with him. I learned how to feel multiple things at once: anxiety and affection, fear and comfort. With him, I wasn't broken. I was complex.

Things were really good with Alex. Like, genuinely good. He was funny and kind, and being with him felt like finding something I didn't know I'd been missing my whole life. So, I kept thinking, *If I have this person—if I'm loved—then everything else should go away, right?* But it didn't. Even when things were going well, I was still checking the backseat of my car. Still looking under the bed. Still walking across campus with that nervous, on-edge energy. I had this amazing, grounded person by my side—someone who made me laugh constantly—and I still felt haunted.

When I was with Alex, though, it was different. I didn't need to look around the corner or double-check locks. He'd walk me to my apartment at night and even come in to make sure everything was okay. He just got it. He didn't make me feel weird about my anxiety—he made me feel safe. He was quirky too, so my quirks weren't a problem.

But intimacy was complicated. It always felt a little off. I had never fully addressed what happened with the older boy, and even though I knew something had happened, I didn't have the words. So, when we were intimate, there was always this undertone—like my body remembered something I hadn't processed yet. I couldn't communicate what felt wrong, because I didn't even understand it myself.

Then there was my mother.

When we'd visit, she was no different with me than she'd ever been, which is to say, distant and cold. And she wasn't openly unkind to Alex, but she also didn't go out of her way to make him feel welcome. It was like he was tolerated, not embraced. There was no warmth, no invitation into the family. Which made no sense—he was smart, successful, polite, and he clearly cared about me. My dad was better. I think he actually liked Alex and tried to connect. Alex would help clear the table and be respectful, but the whole environment still felt ... off. I never once saw my mother make an effort to fully include him as part of our family. And I definitely didn't feel any different in her eyes, even though I was in the healthiest relationship of my life.

Back at school, my group was tight—Alex, my brother, his girlfriend, and a few others. We named our cars. We shared meals. We built little traditions that made life feel less like a performance and more like a life. And yet ... beneath it, the cracks were spreading.

As I moved into my education coursework, studying elementary education, the triggers intensified. Teaching methods, especially for young children, brought back too many memories of my childhood confusion in classrooms, the shame of not understanding, and the fear of being called on. I was thrown back into second grade emotionally while trying to lead a classroom academically. It became unbearable.

So, I developed rituals to manage the anxiety. Obsessive loops. I'd check and re-check things—lights, locks, stove—even though I didn't use the stove. I'd second-guess every step, every word. The compulsion to make sure everything was okay became the thing that made everything not okay.

But one day, during a group project in a math class—ironically about teaching math to second graders—I froze. I didn't understand the material. I couldn't participate. And the shame swallowed me. I excused myself, walked to a campus bathroom, closed the door, and in a haze of panic, took off my belt.

I wasn't trying to die. I was trying to stop the overwhelming rush of noise inside my head. But as soon as I tightened it, I panicked. I called my mother.

Her response? "Why would you do that?"

OTHER VOICES

Brian, My Brother

I think the first time I really sensed something was off with Karen was when she came to visit me during my freshman year of college. She was still in high school, a senior, and I just remember thinking something wasn't right. She wasn't herself. She seemed deeply unhappy and kind of lost. At the time, I couldn't name it. I wasn't trained in mental health, and I was just a college kid. Looking back, maybe there were earlier signs, but that was the moment that stuck with me.

When Karen started going through more serious struggles, I was away at school and didn't know the full picture. Our parents didn't share everything, and I don't blame them for that. They wanted me to focus on my own life. I did come home during one of her hospitalizations, though, and visited her. After that, I tried to check in more often, calling regularly, but I was still very young. I didn't really understand what was happening.

Later on, when she transferred to Ohio State, we lived together for a while. That felt important to me. I wanted to be there, to look out for her. I carried some sense of responsibility—not in a burdensome way, but more as an older brother who cared.

There were definitely moments over the years when it was hard to stay connected—especially when she and Jeff made some choices about her medications that didn't sit well with me. Eventually, she ended up back in the hospital, and I was deeply concerned. But by then, she was an adult, with a husband. I was in Pittsburgh with young children of my own, trying to manage my own life. Still, I kept in touch. During harder periods, I'd call, even if I couldn't get through. I'd leave voicemails just to say I was thinking of her, that I loved her. It became one-sided at times, but I kept doing it.

Not because I expected anything in return. That's just not how I operate. I believe you reach out because it's the right thing to do, not because someone owes you something back. If I send a birthday card or make a call, it's not to keep score. I kept calling because I wanted Karen to know she wasn't forgotten—even when she couldn't respond.

6

~~~~~~~~

THE MANY FACES OF...

THE WORLD SAW a composed, articulate woman with impeccable clothes and enviable poise. At synagogue, she was gracious and admired. In public, she seemed pulled together and competent—an image of suburban success.

But that wasn't the Bev I knew.

Growing up, my mother wasn't one person. She was many. And yet, none of them felt like the mother I needed. Bev was definitely depressed. From what I understand about her father—my grandfather—he was verbally abusive. It's no wonder I never felt completely at ease around him. He had this larger-than-life presence that demanded respect, but not in a healthy way. It was more like: *If you don't respect me, there will be consequences.* I remember my grandmother as more protective—loving in her own way. We didn't spend much time with Bev's parents, so I don't have many clear memories. What stands out are the feelings when I was around them: I felt small and uneasy around my grandfather, but comforted when my grandmother was nearby. You could always tell Bev was uncomfortable in their apartment.

After school, I remember walking home alone the two and a half blocks that felt longer than the school day itself. Other kids would launch themselves into their moms' arms or be greeted by wagging tails when they reached home. I just walked. Past the high school, under the shadow of its walls that loomed like cliffs. I never knew what version of Bev I'd meet when I got home.

The Perfect Mom Who Baked on Fridays

Some moments almost felt like love. Fridays, mostly—Bev's cookie day. Her secret oatmeal chocolate chip recipe was sacred in our house. I loved watching her scrape the mixing blade with just enough precision to leave a little batter behind for my sister and me. It was one of the few customs we shared.

But even those sweet, warm moments came without conversation. There was no *"How was school?"* There was no eye contact. Just the sounds of measuring spoons, clinking dishes, and silence. I learned early that joy in our house came with limits—delivered in careful portions, then wiped away like crumbs.

The Religious Queen of Saturday

There was Synagogue Bev—flawless hair, curled and sprayed. Heels, lipstick, a coordinated suit, and a demeanor that said, *"Look how good I am."* People adored her. But it was theater. She would come alive on Saturday mornings, only to disappear for the rest of the week. They didn't see the Bev who barely left her bedroom, who missed entire days of my life.

I remember being dropped off in the cold basement for the children's service, to be alone and invisible again. When I finally earned the right to sit beside my dad in the main sanctuary, I felt peace for the first time. Until Bev shushed me for whispering. It felt like losing something precious in public—like being scolded for needing love.

The Buckeye Fan I Secretly Preferred

Football Bev might've been my favorite—if only because she wasn't around. On game days, she and my dad became Ohio State (OSU) superfans, and Brian, Malinda, and I finally had the house to ourselves. No judgment. No icy glances. Just peace.

Bev had a degree from OSU, but she'd started and stopped school when she married Ed. Years later, she finished—earning not just a bachelor's but a master's in social work (MSW). She worked with unwed mothers and climbed her way through corporate departments at Marshall Fields. I respected what she accomplished. But I couldn't reach the part of her that knew how to love her daughter.

The Loving Wife Who Saved Affection for Dad

Bev showed affection, but it was reserved for my dad. Before their Saturday night outings, she would descend the stairs like a movie star—perfumed, perfect hair, and in an elegant dress. Dad would fetch her fur coat and place it gently over her shoulders like a ritual. She'd then kiss us goodbye like a formality and vanish into the night.

To the outside eye, she was radiant. But it always felt like a scene from a play that didn't include us in the script.

The Shopping Mom I Dreaded

Shopping with Bev wasn't about fun or bonding—it was about looking presentable. Or more accurately, her version of presentable. When I looked into the fitting room mirrors, all I saw was disapproval. No matter what I tried on, I didn't fit the mold.

There was one exception. A pair of knickers at Burlington Coat Factory. I loved them, and she let me have them. I still remember the shock of hearing her say *yes*.

She didn't go with me to pick out my wedding dress. My soon-to-be mother-in-law, Francie, and some friends stepped in. When Bev finally saw it, she didn't smile. She paid for it like it was an obligation—guilt wrapped in a checkbook. Later, at my sister's wedding, she bought Malinda gifts, lavished her in approval, and expected me to pay for the bridesmaid dress that I couldn't afford. Her favoritism was never subtle.

The Woman Behind the Bedroom Door

When I was in elementary school, Bev lived in her room most of the time. It was her fortress. She'd come out only to make dinner for dad—always perfectly timed—then vanish again. I wasn't allowed in. I wasn't even allowed to eat in my own room.

The house felt empty without her presence. And heavier with it.

I passed the time with my OCD rituals. Reorganizing my room. Refolding clothes. Recoloring order into chaos. Homework blurred into nothing. Time slowed. I waited for my dad's car like it was salvation.

Sometimes, when they were gone for Saturday Ohio State games, I'd sneak into her closet. Everything was lined up with precision—her shoes, her jewelry. I'd stand there, just staring. Scared to touch anything. Desperate to understand the person behind the door.

She Never Broke the Cycle

Bev had a strained relationship with her mother. I never went to my grandparents' funerals. We never talked about them. When we visited Cleveland, the air felt thick, like a storm was always threatening.

Her mother had once been her protector, until time made her too weak to sustain the role. Bev never forgave her for that. And she never stopped punishing me for her disappointment. Unfortunately, Bev didn't break the cycle. She passed it on.

I used to believe the way Bev treated me was a reflection of my shortcomings. That if I had been more obedient, more talented, more lovable, maybe she would have chosen to show up for me. Now, I understand that her behavior wasn't about who I was—it was about who she couldn't be.

OTHER
VOICES   *Gilli, My Son*

I'm Gilli, Karen's oldest son.

To be honest, I don't really remember a clear first moment when I realized something was wrong with my mom's mental health. I just have scattered memories from that time, as it was a long time ago, and I was pretty young. But I knew something was off, even if I didn't understand what it was.

From seventh grade through the middle of high school, things at home were very different. My mom spent most of her time in her room. When I got home from school, I'd be on my own. If my dad wasn't home from work, I basically had free rein. Looking back, I realize there was a real lack of parenting, but at the time, I just thought, "Cool, I can do whatever I want."

During COVID, things didn't feel too different in that regard. I was home all day on Zoom school, stuck in my room doing class after class. After school, it was the same—no parental presence unless my dad was around. And back then, I wasn't very into school, so the lack of supervision gave me more freedom than I probably should have had. It felt great in the moment, but in hindsight, I think I could've used more structure during those years.

I rarely saw my mom during that time. She was just ... in her room. I didn't really know what to make of it, and no one told me the full story. I think I've mentally blocked out a lot of that time. Even now, I'm not sure I ever got the full picture.

When she got better—when they found the right medication—it was like a light switch flipped. Suddenly, she was present again and back in my life. It was honestly confusing. I had spent four years figuring out how to take care of myself, how to structure my day, how to be independent—and then suddenly, I had a parent again, someone stepping in and trying to be involved. It felt like a stranger was trying to parent me. Not in a mean way— just in a jarring, disorienting way.

However, I was happy to have her back, and we have a good relationship now. I love her and I can remember all the memories from when I was younger. But the emotional shift was massive. Nobody around me seemed to acknowledge what had happened. It was like the past four years didn't exist to them, but they did for me. I had changed a lot in that time, and it felt like my mom had missed all of it.

I think some distance is inevitable when someone is gone— emotionally or physically—during such crucial years. When I'm upset or dealing with something personal, I tend to turn to my friends rather than my parents. That's just how I adapted.

Even after learning it was depression, I didn't blame my mom. I never thought she didn't want to be there for us, as it was clear something was blocking her from being able to. Knowing the name of it—severe depression—didn't change much for me emotionally. I had already come to terms with the fact that it was something outside her control.

If I had to give advice to someone else going through something like this, I'd say: "Take care of yourself. As much as you want to fix it or understand it, you won't be able to. What you can do is focus on your own mental and physical well-being. It's not your fault. Blaming yourself is only going to make things harder, and it won't help anyone."

My relationship with my mom now is solid. We talk often—every other day when I'm at school. Every Friday night, she calls to give me the Shabbat blessing. We've taken trips together, too. One of the most meaningful was when we went to Israel in late 2023 to volunteer after the October 7 attacks. That trip was actually her idea. She called me one day and said she felt drawn to go, and she asked if I wanted to come. I said yes immediately. That trip brought us closer.

7

THE STORM BEFORE THE SUN

"Why did you do that?" Bev asked.

No panic. No urgency. Just that one question. It echoed in my ears louder than the fluorescent buzz of the campus bathroom where I had just tried to strangle myself with a belt. I had called her because I didn't know who else to call. Because even when you've been raised in a cold house, sometimes the only number that comes to mind is your mother's.

She picked me up. No embrace. No tears. No conversation. Just a redirect: *"We're going straight to your therapist."*

But it wasn't just another session. That day became the fork in the road. I was hospitalized not long after. It wasn't the first time I'd struggled, but it was the first time anyone named it: OCD. My whole life suddenly had a category.

At the time, I didn't even know what OCD was. I didn't

fit the mold of someone who washed their hands fifty times a day. Mine looked different. It was an invisible ritual: thoughts that wouldn't let go, mental loops that hijacked reality.

The obsession that I was dealing with at the time? The thought that I was a lesbian. Not because I actually was—but because that's how OCD works. It latches on to something personal, and then it won't shut up about it. I didn't understand that back then. I thought I was broken in a new way.

All those years I'd spent rearranging the glass animals on my dresser shelf, color-coding my clothes, counting steps on the sidewalk, avoiding cracks like they'd split my soul open—those weren't quirks. That wasn't me being organized or anxious. It was survival. It was compulsion. It was an illness.

At the facility, they gave me space to draw. During art therapy, someone finally said, *"You should be angry at your mom."* I didn't understand why at the time. They suggested I try drawing what anger looks like. I was given a large sheet of white paper and a black oil crayon. I just started covering the page in black, and slowly, the bright white surface turned into what I imagined anger might look like.

They put me on medication. Not selective serotonin reuptake inhibitors (SSRIs), as those had already failed me. They gave me Nardil. It's a monoamine oxidase (MAOI) inhibitor, old school and heavy duty. A last resort kind of med. The side effects were intense. I was told I couldn't get pregnant on it. I was told to watch my diet, avoid certain foods. But for the first time, the fog started to lift. My brain had been drowning for years, and this medication was like finally surfacing for air.

I wasn't happy. Not even close. But I could think. I could participate in a conversation. I could breathe. For the first time in forever, my brain had a pause in the obsessive loop. I wasn't stuck repeating mantras just to make it down the hallway or berating myself while trying to get through college homework. It was like the record needle finally skipped just enough to break the cycle, and for a few moments, there was silence. No compulsions. No self-hate. Just quiet.

When I left the hospital, I thought maybe things would change. But Bev didn't want me back in the house. So, I moved into an apartment in Bexley Square. My friends helped me with the move. Alex stayed with me during all of this. He didn't walk away. But I did. Quietly. I detached. I knew I couldn't carry the relationship and the illness at the same time. When he got into medical school, I went with him to visit. We were in a hallway, and I had a moment of complete clarity—*I can't do this. I can't go with him. I'm not okay.* I had to let him go, even though he never asked me to. Even though it broke my heart. Letting go of Alex was one of the hardest things I've ever done. He was the first person who made me feel like I wasn't broken. But I didn't believe I could hold on to him and still survive myself. And part of me honestly believed I didn't deserve that kind of love anyway.

After that, I continued with school and tried to keep going, but soon, I realized I couldn't even take care of myself. I don't even remember how everything fell apart, but one night, I couldn't be by myself and felt like I couldn't sleep at the apartment anymore.

So, I rang the doorbell at my parents' house.

Everyone who ever came to our house used the front door. I always loved its unique round top; it felt like a distinctive feature. But it also felt like a gate to the hidden world of our family. The heavy, dark main door, paired with the screen door, was anything but inviting. Even though it was my home, it felt strange to approach that door and ring the doorbell. You'd think that someone who had lived in a house most of her life would just go to the back door and walk right in. But that wasn't an option for me—not then. There was no real sense of welcome or warmth waiting behind that fortress.

I remember my dad being the one to open the door, with Bev standing behind him. We spoke through the screen door—I wasn't even invited into the foyer to ask for help during what was clearly a crisis. I told Ed I had nowhere to sleep that night. For a moment, it seemed like he might open the door and let me in ... but then something stopped him. There was a look. Bev's signature look that meant absolutely not. The kind of look that carried an unspoken ultimatum, one that everyone in our house recognized. It said: Be *careful how you handle this—if you get too close to her, there will be consequences.* I watched as the heavy, dark door slowly closed. I believe the two of them spoke briefly behind it. Then Ed reopened the door and said, "You can stay at a hotel."

I remember walking away from that fortress to my car, which wasn't even parked in the driveway, but out on the street, where guests or strangers park. I got in and drove straight to my friend Ronit's apartment on the Ohio State campus. All I had to do was ring the outside buzzer, and I was immediately welcomed into safety and security—no questions asked. That's what I did. I survived by finding places to land.

It was my fifth year—the one where student teaching was supposed to pull everything together. I was just out of the hospital, newly diagnosed, on new meds, and barely stitched together emotionally. Functioning, yes. But underneath? I was still struggling.

And then I met Mrs. Allison.

She was this tiny woman with an enormous presence. Her presence was like Ms. Barbara's, my kindergarten teacher. Mrs. Allison was more reserved yet just as loving at the same time. Her classroom was magical—soft, tactile, alive with color and warmth. Everything in it was built for connection and safety. It wasn't just for the kids. It was for me, too.

Mrs. Allison was the kind of teacher who saw every child, no, really saw them. She met each kid exactly where they were with no judgment, just compassion and intention. I wasn't just watching her teach; I was learning how to be a person again. Her room gave me something I didn't know I needed—structure and softness, side by side.

And I thrived. Because someone was there. Because I wasn't alone.

Yet, at the same time, I was completely triggered. Being around five-year-olds brought me right back to being seven. To the attic. To the silence. I would teach with a smile on my face and walk out feeling like a child who needed to hide in her closet. I was successful, but I also regressed. I knew what to do with the kids, how to explain math, how to connect—but inside, I was still that scared little girl looking for someone to protect her.

Mrs. Allison became something like a mother figure to me—only a safe one. Someone who showed up every day and didn't flinch. I didn't even realize how much I needed that until I was standing in her classroom. She probably had no idea. But she was one of the people who helped me remember I was capable of showing up, even when it hurt.

Then the end of the semester came, my last year in college. Student teaching ended along with my consistent routine, which was essential to my stability. I remember graduation, but only in pieces. My siblings weren't there; my brother was working in Jacksonville, Florida, and my sister was an undergrad at the University of Miami. There was no celebration, no hugs, no sense of completion—just Bev and Ed taking me to lunch like it was any other errand. I felt completely hollow. Like I had crossed some kind of finish line, but no one was watching, and I wasn't even sure what I'd finished.

Afterward, I somehow got a teaching job in a good school district. Ironically, the same one I had graduated from, the Bexley City School District. Honestly, I have no idea how I passed the interview. But I had incredible recommendations. I also taught first grade at my synagogue, and I thrived there. A big part of that was because of a woman named Donna. She taught me Hebrew before I ever started teaching it. We'd sit together, and she'd tutor me. She was patient, supportive, and kind. Ironically, she was also a close friend of my mother's, which made things ... complicated, but she never let that get in the way. Donna became another maternal figure in my life. I even babysat for her kids. At Hebrew school, I was confident. I nailed it. I was a really, really fantastic teacher. And it all came from this belief she and Mrs. Allison taught me: Every student deserves the opportunity to learn and be loved. That doesn't sound so hard—but in the right environment, it's everything.

Even so, nothing felt safe—not my apartment, not the school, not even myself. I had two different apartments the year after graduation. One was with a woman named Deb, whose massive dog destroyed the floor on a regular basis. I couldn't bring myself to leave, though. I couldn't even do basic lesson plans. But I kept showing up to classes, because that's what I'd always known: just push through. Push through I did, and things managed to settle down.

I dated Joey, a guy I met through a BBYO friend. He used recreational drugs, which was not my thing, but his mom was kind to me, and at that point, that was enough. I didn't care about red flags—I just wanted someone to make me feel like I mattered.

Then Jeff called. He had been a crush since I was fifteen in BBYO, and now he was calling to tell me he had feelings for me. I immediately broke things off with Joey and drove to Indiana to be with Jeff. Bloomington felt like a place I could vanish into. Being with Jeff made me feel normal. When we were together, I felt more whole. Yet, just like at camp, where I used to count down the days until I had to go home, I did the same with Jeff. Our time together was limited to short weekends, and even on Friday afternoons, as soon as I arrived in Bloomington, I was already dreading the Sunday drive back to Columbus—back to being completely alone.

I was living a double life—performing the part of someone who had it together, while privately unraveling. The rest of the year, I was teaching. Barely. By February, I met with the principal and told him I didn't know if I could finish the school year. He said I could stay or leave. However, I didn't have the option of quitting because I couldn't go to

Bev and Ed for help; there would be none. So, I stayed, even though some days I didn't have lesson plans, just vague ideas and survival mode. When I taught second grade, honestly, I should've never made it through. Thankfully, two other second-grade teachers who had been in the system for years offered to team-teach with me—split responsibilities to support each other. But for some reason, I said no. I thought I had to prove something, or maybe fix it my way. Which, looking back, was a really bad decision.

I had this idea that I was going to reinvent everything. I didn't want to teach from a workbook where you just write the question, then write the answer. I wanted everything to be hands-on—manipulatives, touchable, visual, and interactive. I thought that was what good teaching looked like. And maybe it was, in theory. But I also had no structure. I didn't accept the help that was offered. I saw those veteran teachers as stuck, boring, and too traditional. I was convinced I could do it better.

I probably should've said yes to the help.

I wasn't asked back.

I cried to Jeff on the phone more than once. Columbus didn't feel like home. It didn't feel like anything. Eventually, I faced a decision—stay stuck, or try something new. Jeff was moving to Florida. My first cousin was in Atlanta and distant relatives lived in Florida. I wasn't strong enough for either, but I had to do something. I chose Florida.

Ronit, My Friend Since College

Karen and I met my very first week at Ohio State, in the fall of 1991. We were in the same Spanish class, but we also met separately through mutual friends, and we just clicked. She was a year ahead of me and had transferred in. From that moment on, we've remained friends through every stage: college, post-college, her relationship with Jeff, having kids, everything. I've witnessed nearly every phase of her illness, from early signs in college to some of her lowest points.

The first time I really became aware of Karen's mental health struggles was when she told me. I don't think I recognized any signs myself. I just remember that during our college years, she was hospitalized. It must have been my junior year. She took some quarters off and was really in a dark place. At one point, she told me she had been suicidal and even homicidal. That shocked me, especially because this was the early '90s—people didn't talk openly about mental illness.

I remember visiting her when she moved in with one of her father's hygienists. I'd go over to her place, bring ice cream, watch movies, just try to be present. Then later, she had a period where she was living alone near her parents' house and was very suicidal. I'll never forget that apartment. That time is etched in my memory.

After college, I moved to Israel, and when I came back to Columbus, she had moved to Florida with Jeff. Not long after, she got very sick again and came back to Ohio. That's when she was hospitalized in a state facility—and that was extremely hard. I was only twenty-three at the time, working at the Jewish Community Center (JCC), living on my own. I had never been to a state institution before. It was bleak and sterile, and it confused me. Karen came from a family with means—her father was a doctor— and I couldn't understand why she wasn't in a private facility.

During those months, I visited her three times a week— sometimes on my lunch break, sometimes after work. She was heavily medicated and not always communicative. I don't even think she remembers much of that time. It was traumatic for me. I remember once a friend of hers flew in to visit and stayed with me. We went to the hospital together and ended up washing Karen's hair in the bathroom sink. That's where she was—unable to care for herself, and in a very bad state.

Through it all, I stuck by her. Karen had always been a generous, kind, loving friend, and I never forgot that. I knew that the woman I saw during those dark periods wasn't all of her. I'd seen her get better before, and I held onto that hope. I wasn't trying to fix her because I knew that wasn't my role. But I wanted her to know she wasn't alone.

Looking back, I wish I'd gotten therapy earlier. Some of it was really traumatic—especially being asked by her parents to move in with her because they were afraid she might take her own life. I was just twenty-one years old. I remember calling my parents, and they were horrified. That kind of responsibility at that age ... it was overwhelming.

One of the biggest things I've learned through this friendship is that being there for someone doesn't mean they'll always be happy to see you, or even respond. When I visited Karen in the hospital, she wasn't always glad to see me. That wasn't the point. I wasn't doing it to feel better about myself—I was doing it so she wouldn't be alone. Even if she couldn't process it, I was showing up. That mattered to me.

Karen is a very intense friend—fiercely loyal, deeply emotional. There were times, years later, when she called me out because she felt disconnected from me. And she wasn't wrong. I was a single parent working full time, running nonprofits, navigating a lot—but when she said it, I heard her. And I recommitted. That's just who she is—she doesn't let go of people she loves.

Today, our relationship is good. We don't talk constantly, but we're in each other's lives. She came to my kids' b'nai mitzvah, made a huge effort to show up. I've been to Kansas City for work and always made a point to see her.

She embraces every day with intention now, and I think, in part, she's trying to make up for some of the time she lost when she was unwell.

If I had to give advice to someone supporting a friend with mental illness, it would be this: Get your own support. You're not supposed to solve it. Being a friend isn't the same as being a therapist. You can't fix them. But you can show up. You can bear witness. And you can do it without expecting anything in return.

Mental illness is not something that just goes away. It's like a scar—it might fade, but it never fully disappears. It becomes part of who you are. Most days, it doesn't hurt. But every once in a while, something rubs against it—a memory, a trigger, a moment of stress—and it reminds you that the pain was real. Karen has carried her scars for a long time. I've seen her fall, and I've seen her heal. And I've seen her walk through the world with strength, even when those old wounds start to sting.

I've also learned that you never really know what someone else has been through. People see Karen now—active in the community, present, vibrant—and they have no idea what it took for her to get here.

But I do.

And I'm proud to still be standing beside her.

8

IT HAPPENED AGAIN

JEFF WAS GOING to be in Florida, and I was very lucky—I had cousins there. My dad's first cousins had all grown up together with him in Cleveland. My grandmother and her brother lived in a duplex: my dad's family lived upstairs, and her brother's family lived downstairs. My great-aunt Rose and Uncle Herman—my dad's aunt and uncle—had three sons: Marty, Jerry, and Ronnie. They were like siblings to my dad and his sisters. The families did everything together; they even worked together.

Eventually, all three—Ronnie, Jerry, and Marty—ended up in Florida, and their families were based there. I had a special bond with Ronnie and his wife, Eileen. Ronnie was the middle brother, and he and Eileen became like parents to me. When I first moved to Florida, my apartment wasn't ready yet, so I stayed at their home. They knew a lot—my history, my parents, the dynamics. Even now, they're still a part of my life. They've continued to support me through everything. I would honestly consider them as close to parents as anyone has ever been.

Also living in Florida at the time were my grandma Goldie and her sister, Aunt Rose. Jeff and I would visit them regularly—about twice a month. Because they were older, and we both had tiny sports cars, we had to carefully help them into the seats before taking them to dinner. I loved those outings. I loved having them close.

I eventually started interviewing for a teaching position, and Jeff came into town to go with me. We drove around Broward County. One interview was at a modern Orthodox day school where kids walked between classrooms outside. It felt strange. Foreign. But also kind of exciting. I ended up accepting a position at another Jewish day school teaching second grade. And Jeff pursued finishing a medical rotation on a base in Biloxi, Mississippi, so he was no longer in Florida full time.

I then got a two-bedroom apartment, hoping I'd find a roommate. I signed the lease on my own, which felt bold at the time. I brought a couch from home. A bed. A few things.

At first, it was good. My coworkers were older, kind. There was one woman, warm and Southern, who felt like a mom. She invited me to her house. She made it feel like I belonged. I had a real classroom. I was teaching. Functioning. I remember introducing the vocabulary word "rake" and watching the kids stare back at me blankly because in Florida, there were no seasons. No leaves. No raking.

Around this time, I also became deeply involved with BBYO. I soon met Ali—one of those instant, soul-level friendships. I even became an adviser for a BBYO girls' chapter. That was another way I connected with families, many of whom I later babysat for. Ali and I took a cooking class, got professional photos together, and once had to perform emergency hair surgery after she got a brush stuck in hers. It was that kind of friendship.

The people I worked with were kind, but they had their lives. I did build some relationships with families from the school. On weekends, I would often babysit when parents were traveling or working. Nevertheless, my roommate was absent, but the geckos weren't. Jeff told me to stuff a towel under the door at night so they wouldn't come crawling in through the crack. So, I did.

Three months later, Jeff finished his rotation and drove straight to me. I remember we made popcorn and sat on the couch and watched something on TV. I don't remember what it was. I just remember the popcorn and him beside me. It felt like hope. Not long after Jeff arrived, we got engaged. He proposed on Fort Lauderdale Beach. I wasn't in the best mood—it was chilly, and I was being stubborn about walking on the beach. But he got me there, and he asked. I said *yes*. Then we drove to Grandma Goldie's apartment to show her the ring. She was thrilled. Later, with

Eileen, Aunt Sheila, and Francie, I even found my wedding dress—without Bev, which didn't go over well. But the people who showed their love for me were there, and that's what mattered.

And for a while, I felt good.

Not euphoric. Not invincible. Just … steady. I was showing up. I was doing the job. I had a little routine—teaching, coming home, spending time with Jeff if he had time. I'd drive with the windows down. The sky felt big. I was proud of my classroom. I had coworkers who respected me. I remember thinking, *maybe this is what normal looks like.* And because of this, I made the classic mistake: I took myself off Nardil. Jeff and I thought maybe I didn't need it anymore and didn't consult a doctor. I had been on Nardil since my early twenties, and we just … stopped. It was late January, maybe early February. Cold turkey.

That's when everything began to quietly unravel.

It was a slow progression—like the adult part of me was slipping away, piece by piece. Time felt suspended, like everything was moving in slow motion. I was trying so hard to stay functional, to stay adult, but I could feel myself reverting to a younger version of myself—scared, unsure, and needing care. I remember one day in particular. I went to work not feeling well, yet trying to push through. Eventually, I had to leave school early, and I got sick on the way home. I can still see it clearly—coming back to my apartment, standing there, unsure of what to do. Soon after, I stopped functioning. I stopped going to work. I stopped getting out of bed.

Jeffry noticed and called my parents. They flew out.

Bev walked into my room and said, *"Get up; let's get you on a plane to our house so you can regroup and then fly back home."* Like it was that simple. Like all I needed was to pack a bag and have a weekend away. Then Bev and Jeff fought about it. Jeff wanted to oversee my care, and have me stay in Florida, but my parents were not having that. Bev wanted it over with.

OTHER VOICES

Ron and Eileen,
My Family in Florida, Cousins

Ron: *Karen's father is my first cousin. We grew up together in the same house in Cleveland when we were kids. As adults, though, we lost touch. I moved to Florida with Eileen in our twenties, and he made his life in Columbus. Other than the occasional family update, we weren't really in contact—until Karen called out of the blue.*

She was thinking about relocating to Florida and wanted to understand the Jewish community down here—Federation, JCC, that sort of thing. At the time, I was active on the board of Federation and very involved in Jewish philanthropy. Karen and I didn't really know each other, but one conversation led to another, and before we knew it, she came to stay with us while she got settled.

Eileen: *It's funny because she initially wanted to speak with me about Jewish organizations, even though Ron was the one heavily involved, not me. Still, we immediately formed a bond. She stayed in our home, and even though we hadn't known each other beforehand, it felt natural. We became close—like surrogate parents, or an aunt and uncle. She was part of our lives in Florida.*

Eventually, Karen got an apartment with a roommate we helped connect her with. But it didn't work out too well—the roommate was usually away at her boyfriend's, and

Karen spent a lot of time alone. Over time, we started to notice signs that she was struggling. She shared with us that she had mental health issues and was on medication. For a while, she seemed stable, but then there was a clear downturn.

Ron: *I got in touch with her father, and eventually, Karen was hospitalized. I can't recall exactly where or when, but I do remember that she wasn't doing well. Later on, Jeff came down to Florida for his fellowship at Bascom Palmer Eye Institute, and we maintained our connection with both of them. Even when they moved to Kansas City, we stayed in touch.*

Eileen: *I'll never forget when Karen asked me and Jeff's mother to go wedding dress shopping with her. Not her own mother—us. That said a lot about the kind of connection we had, and about her relationship with her mom. I felt for her. I think her mother was very controlling. I don't know all the details, but I could see that they just didn't have that mother-daughter bond.*

Ron: *Karen was like family to us. She confided in us. We listened. We cared. Even when she moved away, we'd stop through Kansas City on road trips and grab a meal with her and Jeff. I remember a time when she and the boys came back from a cruise and stayed with us. She went straight to bed and barely got up. She was clearly in the midst of another episode. Her youngest must've* been around seven. I took the boys out. We did our best to make them feel safe.

Eileen: *That visit broke my heart. She was in so much pain. I didn't know what to do except be there. Love her. Hug her. Make sure the boys were okay. We were in touch with Jeff the whole time, but it's hard to know what to do in those moments. When someone you love is in crisis, and you're not a professional, all you can offer is your presence.*

Ron: *Our philosophy was, we're here, we love her, and if something serious is happening, we make sure the right people—Jeff, her dad—know. We weren't trying to fix anything we weren't qualified to fix. But we were always there to be a safe place.*

Eileen: *My advice for supporting someone with mental illness would be: listen, don't judge, and offer your love. And get help from professionals when needed. My own mother struggled with mental illness, so I had some sense of the ups and downs. I knew how isolating and frightening it can be—for everyone involved.*

Ron: *And we'd add, don't underestimate the value of just being present. You might not be able to fix anything, but your care matters. Sometimes, that's what gets someone through.*

9

COMING HOME,
BUT NOT REALLY HOME

NONE OF US knew that going off the MAOI had triggered the spiral. Not yet. But that moment was the beginning of the next descent.

When I got back to Columbus, my parents put me in the attic, which was on a different floor from Bev's room, which I think was the reason. The attic was my sister's room. It wasn't my space. It was also in an attic where I had been sexually assaulted as a child. Being placed there—not asked, just put there—felt like another violation. I wasn't functioning. I wasn't safe.

Coming back from Florida felt less like returning home and more like stepping into a carefully constructed plan that wasn't mine. From the start, Bev made it clear: I was going to see the therapist she and my dad had chosen, and I was going to get better—quickly. Inpatient treatment wasn't an option. Not because I didn't need it, but because they weren't going to pay for it. That was the turkey burger. There was no beef burger. No menu. Just one option—and it wasn't optional.

I started therapy, but nothing was improving. I wasn't getting out of bed. I wasn't on the right medication. I had completely regressed mentally and emotionally—I wasn't twenty-two; I was five. But to my parents, that wasn't acceptable. The message was clear: Get a grip, go to therapy, get better, and get out. Because Bev's house wasn't my house. I wasn't part of the family—I was a guest. An unwanted one.

The therapist they picked used Gestalt methods—focusing on present moment awareness and self-responsibility. The idea was that I'd sit across from someone, maybe Jeff, and express what I was feeling in real time. But I wasn't feeling anything. I was too far gone to be present. The therapy wasn't helping. However, twice a week, I'd drag myself out of bed and go. I wasn't improving, and no one seemed to care so long as I was checking the therapy box.

Eventually, I knew I had to make my own choice. I wasn't getting better, and no one else was going to help me. The only way out was to leave. Not in rebellion, but in survival. I figured out a path back to care. Back to myself. It wasn't easy, and I don't give myself enough credit for it, but looking back, that moment—deciding I couldn't live like that anymore—was the beginning of reclaiming my life.

I called the police. I told the officer I was a danger to myself and others. They took me to the Ohio State Mental Facility.

Five months. No therapy. No insight. Just structure: meals, required physical activity, and basic hygiene. The psychiatrist ran me through various SSRIs, which didn't work for me. But eventually, they restarted the Nardil, and within a few weeks, the dull weight in my brain slowly began to shift. Medication is a strange thing. It's not a cure or a personality transplant. It's scaffolding. When it's right, it makes it possible to be who you are. When it's wrong, it pushes you further into the dark. I've been on both sides.

Visits to the mental health facility were always a bit surreal. Some people came because they genuinely cared, others because they didn't know what else to do. My dad would walk with me in the garden or down the hallway—quietly, cautiously—like he was afraid of breaking something fragile. Jeff visited when he could, steady and present, never making me feel like I was too much. Bev came too, but those visits were strained. When we walked, she kept her distance—literally trailing ten steps behind me and my dad, like she couldn't bring herself to join us. The divide wasn't just physical; it was emotional. The visits weren't comforting—they were reminders of how far I'd fallen and how uncertain everything still was. But even in those moments, I was beginning to understand who felt safe, and who didn't.

When I left the hospital, I had nothing. My apartment in

Florida had been emptied. My belongings ended up being stolen from my car, where I was storing my things. Now all I had were the clothes I walked out with.

But there was no option to return to my parents' house. Jeff and I weren't together at the time, and our engagement was on hold. But I couldn't live alone. My brother was married, and my sister was likely out of the country. So, Aunt Shush and Uncle Neal took me in. I drove two and a half hours to Cleveland the same day I was discharged. It was crazy. But it was the only option.

I had Aunt Shush. I had Cleveland. I had time.

In Cleveland, I started to heal. I worked part-time at The Cooker, a restaurant I loved. It was right near Grandma Goldie's apartment, and I'd see her three times a week. She was calm and wise. She was aware of the caustic family dynamic, and she had made peace with her son, whom she loved, and his wife, anyway. I'd sleep over sometimes, make her a faux cocktail—Sprite and cranberry juice—and we'd just sit and talk. That time mattered. It was the first time in a long time I felt needed and loved at the same time.

Reconnecting on Thanksgiving

After my time in Cleveland, I spent Thanksgiving with Jeff's family, just as I had many times before. But this visit felt different. It was the first time I saw him since he came to the hospital. Something about being in that familiar space, upstairs in one of the rooms, allowed us to drop the pretense and really connect again. That day, we quietly re-engaged—not with a ring or an announcement, but with a shared understanding that we were going to try again. This time for real.

The plan was simple: I would move to Kansas City in late December. But not into Jeff's place, as he already had a roommate, and she made it clear she wasn't interested in having a third person move in. So, I had to figure it out on my own. I needed two things: a job and a place to live.

The job came quickly. I was hired as the teacher for the after-school care program at the local JCC. That part felt grounding, almost comforting—it gave me purpose and a place to go each day. However, finding housing was more of a challenge. The only roommate I could find was a woman whose name I can't even remember now, but she was... strange. She lived on the Missouri side in a tiny, old house that had a basement that felt more like a set from a horror movie than a new beginning.

Yet, I tried to make it work. But there were things—little things—that just unsettled me. She reused paper napkins, which I found oddly disturbing. And the basement, where the laundry was, felt like it belonged in an eighty-year-old haunted house. It gave me the creeps every time I had to go down there, but I didn't have much of a choice. I was there to build a life, and that meant tolerating the bizarre so I could move forward.

Then by the following summer—either June or July of 1998—Jeff's lease ended, and we moved in together. That felt like the real start of something. We stayed in Kansas City, began to build a shared life, and by February 1999, we were married. The wedding took place at my childhood synagogue in Columbus, Tifereth Israel. It was a beautiful event, but looking back, it was really Bev's wedding. She had her fingerprints all over it. In hindsight, we probably should've just taken the money and run, but at the time, it was the expected thing to do.

Jeffry, My Husband

We first met through BBYO in high school—same region, Kentucky, Indiana, and Ohio. I went to a regional meeting in Dayton, Ohio, by chance, and that's where we first connected. We were juniors. But we didn't date then; we became close friends first. Back in those days, we wrote actual letters—like with stamps—and we did that for years. We were each other's confidants. We knew everything about each other's lives—boyfriends, girlfriends, hopes, frustrations. But we didn't start dating until I was in my fourth year of optometry school—nearly a decade later.

Looking back, I've thought a lot about when I first realized something was going on with Karen's mental health. It's hard to pinpoint. I remember visiting her childhood home in high school—the vacuumed carpet with the perfect lines made an impression—but I don't remember much else about her parents then. During college, we didn't see each other much. The first real time I saw something up close was in Florida.

Karen was living in Fort Lauderdale, and I was in Miami. She had a good job, a few close friends, and her grandmother was nearby, with whom she was really close. Things seemed stable. And then—suddenly—it wasn't. It was a total breakdown. I was shocked at how fast everything unraveled. At first, I tried to convince her to stay, but she was just not functioning. Her parents came to take her back to Ohio. Not long after that, she was hospitalized. That was tough. We were engaged at the time. I remember going to see her once while she was hospitalized, but contact was really limited. Honestly, I probably tried to suppress a lot of that time. It was painful for both of us.

That first engagement is kind of a funny story, though. We had dinner with her grandmother and aunt, and afterward, I tried to get her to go for a walk on the beach. She didn't want to. She was cold and annoyed. I practically dragged her onto the sand—she was full-on pissed—and in the middle of all that, I proposed. Somehow, she still said yes. We laugh about that a lot now.

We never completely disconnected after her hospitalization, but things were distant. Her parents took over—understandably, I guess—and I think they felt a strong sense of responsibility for her well-being. I was just a grad student. Still, there was this lingering feeling that they treated her like something fragile, and I wasn't sure how to re-enter that space.

A few years later, we got re-engaged. Same ring. Much less drama. More of a mutual decision—we were still together, she was doing better, and it felt like it was time. From that point on, I've been there through it all. There were parts of her story I wasn't present for, like her childhood, but everything since our teens—I've seen firsthand, sometimes close up, sometimes from afar.

10

THE FUNCTIONING FIFTEEN

JEFFRY

The one who stayed.

He saw me fall apart—more than once. He saw me disappear into myself and somehow didn't run. He witnessed the spirals, the flatline stretches, the slow-motion collapses, and he stayed. Not just physically. He stayed emotionally. Spiritually. He didn't look away. He fought for me, especially in the moments when I had nothing left to fight with.

And for a long time, I didn't understand why.

That's the thing about mental illness—especially when it's rooted in trauma. It warps your sense of self-worth. When someone shows up for you again and again, you don't feel grateful. You feel suspicious. You wonder what's wrong with them. Why would anyone choose this? Why would anyone choose me? I spent years trying to repay a debt I believed he was collecting. Years feeling like I had to perform, to earn my keep in the relationship. And when I couldn't, I would spiral even more. I would start resenting him, which made me feel even worse. That cycle is cruel. But it's real.

Jeff never made me feel like a burden. That part came entirely from me.

From the outside, our life looked like a success story. We had two kids. A house. I had a good job at the JCC, then the Jewish Federation. I worked with families. I built programs. I ran meetings. I remember standing in front of a room full of community leaders, making a case for our budget, using my voice like I knew what I was doing. And in many ways, I did. I was capable. I was smart. I had gifts. I earned an executive master's in public administration while raising children and working full time. I even worked at First Call, helping people navigate addiction and recovery—while quietly navigating my mental health recovery.

I was high-functioning.

That phrase sounds like praise. It's not. It's camouflage.

Because underneath all that, I was unraveling. Quietly. Constantly. I'd get through a meeting with a donor, write a grant, design a program, lead a training, and still spend the rest of the day locked in obsessive thoughts, trying to keep the panic at bay. There were weeks I survived on fumes. I'd go from presentation to staff meeting to picking up my kids from school. I purposely was living in constant motion with no room to think about feelings and my sickness.

I was doing very well this way. And yet, I had told myself that love—Jeff's love, my kids' love, even my right to exist— was conditional on my ability to hold it all together. This was reinforced by the accolades I received for my work, which didn't make it any easier. And I was barely holding on, which, due to all these factors, prevented me from real- izing this.

There were good seasons, too. Not everything was hard. There were stretches when the medication was working, the therapy was helping, and I felt like I had some traction. I could be present. I could laugh. I could believe, briefly, that maybe I was more than my illness.

Jeff made that possible—not by fixing me, but by stay- ing steady when I couldn't be.

He was steady. Practical. Unwavering. Sometimes I hated him for that. Not because I didn't love him—I did, and I do—but because his steadiness forced me to confront my chaos. He reminded me what consistency looked like. What safety could feel like. And part of me didn't trust it. I didn't believe it could last.

I pushed against it.

There were moments when I wanted him to leave—not because I didn't want him, but because I couldn't bear the weight of being loved like that. I didn't feel worthy of some- one showing up for me again and again without asking for something in return. I didn't know how to receive that kind of love. And it showed.

But he stayed.

He stayed when I withdrew. He stayed when I lashed out. He stayed when I dissociated for days at a time. He stayed when I couldn't get out of bed. He stayed when I couldn't stop crying, and when I couldn't feel anything at all. He stayed even when the version of me I was offering him felt more like a ghost than a wife.

We were raising children in the middle of all this. I was still trying to be a mother. I would show up for school drop-offs, go to therapy, come home and make dinner, then collapse. Jeff picked up the pieces without complaint. He took over when I disappeared. He filled in the blanks I couldn't cover. I don't think I ever thanked him enough. I don't think I ever could.

At First Call, I worked with people in recovery and the loved ones who were impacted, and in those people, I saw versions of myself. The difference was, I was still hiding. My pain was invisible. That made it easier to deny. It also made it harder to get help.

Sometimes I wonder how many other people lived like that—operating at full capacity on the surface, while falling apart underneath. I wasn't alone, but I felt like I was. I think that's one of the most dangerous parts of being high functioning: People don't see it until it's too late. You don't even see it yourself until the foundation gives way.

For fifteen years, I lived a double life. I was capable and crumbling. Professional and paralyzed. Loving and afraid.

I was surviving, and on certain days, even thriving. But underneath it all, I was carrying an unbearable weight. The weight of my past. My illness. My shame.

And Jeff carried it with me.

He didn't try to fix me. He didn't tell me to smile more. He didn't ask why I couldn't just get over it. He just kept showing up.

Even when I wanted to disappear.

Even when I thought I didn't deserve him.

Even when I thought I didn't deserve anything.

Jeff stayed.

Jeffry, My Husband

We've lived through the "black holes" together. That's what we call the worst episodes—Nashville, Wisconsin—those periods were like black holes. You get pulled into something chaotic, mysterious. You don't know what's happening, and when you finally come out the other side, you can't explain what just happened. It's ungraspable. The term stuck. We still use it.

Living with someone who's had breakdowns like that changes you. During those times, it was vital for me to keep some structure. Therapy has never really clicked for me—Karen's always encouraged it, but I haven't found the right person. What helped me was a physical routine. I swim early in the morning, and even when Karen was in treatment, I kept that up. I adjusted it so I could be home in time for the kids. That gave me something to hold onto, especially when everything else was out of my control.

One thing I've learned—and I say this to anyone who loves someone with mental health issues—is that there's a massive difference between everyday struggles and full-on decompensation. Most people with mental health challenges won't go through what Karen did. But when someone does—when they break down completely—it's unpredictable. It's not like a thunderstorm you can wait out. Sometimes it's a drizzle, sometimes a tornado. And you just don't know which it's going to be.

For a long time, I was hypervigilant. I'd come home from swimming and look for signs. If the lights weren't on, I'd panic. I'd assume something was wrong. I'd ask her constantly, "Are you okay?" That's not sustainable—for either of us. I had to learn to stop looking for clues in every little thing. Now, if she says she's not feeling well, I ask, "Physical or emotional?" If it's emotional, I ask, "Should I be concerned?" And most of the time, it's just a bad day. That shift in perspective made a big difference. I had to stop living in the shadow of the last crisis.

And I think that helped our relationship, too. Karen didn't need me constantly hovering. No one wants to feel like they're under surveillance. Once I backed off, we had more room to actually live, and not just brace for the next collapse.

Karen's stronger than most people know. From the outside, people see someone who gets stuff done—because she does. But they don't see the work she puts into staying well. Daily yoga, therapy, mindfulness—none of that is accidental. She's worked as hard on herself as she has on anything else in her life. And she's fiercely committed to helping others, too. This book is a part of that. It's her way of being loud about something most people are quiet about.

11

PARENTING WITHOUT A BLUEPRINT

I NEVER WANTED to become the kind of mother I had. In fact, I spent most of my life insisting that I would not. The first thing to go was saying, "Because I said so." As a child, I would always want to know the answers to questions, and Bev's rote answer would shut me down. I wanted my children to have those answers.

Motherhood was something I wanted, and I knew I would do it differently. I would give my children something that felt like safety, like presence, like love without conditions. Gilli and Eitan weren't just blessings; they were also my second chance. Not to redo my childhood—but to end the cycle that had defined it.

Choosing to Be the Mother I Never Had

In my early 20s, when I was put on Nardil, a powerful MAOI that came with strict dietary restrictions and made getting pregnant more complicated—it was like a blessing in disguise. Inside, I was relieved that my children would be from a different genetic pool—one that would not have the chance to inherit my and my family's mental health issues.

We adopted Gilli in 2003 and Eitan six years later. Becoming a mother this way—by choice, not biology—felt right for me. I had spent so much of my life feeling like I didn't belong anywhere. But I chose them, and I chose the kind of family I wanted to create with Jeff: one where our children knew they were wanted, where their needs were heard, where their voices mattered, and where the absence of my genes would not be a factor.

It wasn't always easy. I didn't have a model to follow. My mother parented through control and criticism. My dad parented with the best intentions when he was available. What I learned growing up was that emotions were threats, needs were nuisances, and love was transactional. My job as a child was to do the right thing—to be polite, smile, never disrupt. That was what love looked like in the house I grew up in: performative obedience.

When I became a mother, I found myself trying to unlearn all of that. I reminded myself, daily, that I didn't have to parent the way I was parented. I didn't have to repeat the patterns that raised me.

Parenting While Managing Mental Health

Motherhood didn't erase my mental illness. It just gave me more reasons to fight it.

There were days I couldn't hide my struggle—when OCD or depression made it hard to function. But I tried to stay honest with my kids in age-appropriate ways. I never wanted them to feel responsible for my well-being. I just wanted them to know that I was human—and that being human didn't make me unsafe.

The Line Between Protection and Projection

Parenting didn't come with a manual—but even if it had, I probably would have second-guessed it. I often felt caught between wanting to protect my kids and not knowing when my past was influencing my reactions more than the present.

With Eitan, our youngest son, I could see this clearly. There was a boy at his school—possibly on the spectrum, maybe with Tourette's—who had social quirks and sometimes repeated things that made Eitan laugh. The first time he came home laughing about it, I jumped in right away: "That's not nice." I couldn't even let him have that moment of fifteen-year-old humor without trying to teach a lesson. Maybe it was the right instinct. Maybe it was too much.

Another time, his friend's mom called to say Eitan had

said something that hurt his friend's feelings. I overcorrected again. I made Eitan apologize in person and told him they couldn't hang out unsupervised. I arranged a forced bonding experience—an escape room—with both dads present, hoping to engineer kindness into their friendship. It was my way of managing the discomfort, of trying to fix things before they got messy. But I know now I was responding as much to my anxiety as to their behavior.

With Gilli, I see different patterns. He once got in trouble for locking a girl out of the senior lounge. Her father called it emotionally abusive. That word sent alarm bells off in my head. I wanted to make sure he wasn't crossing lines, but I also knew he was reacting out of frustration. I didn't think he was being cruel—he was seventeen, and she wasn't listening to him. Still, her father called me before they left for a school trip to Israel, essentially to warn me to keep my son in line. I told him plainly: "If you're worried about your daughter, you might want to make sure *she's* behaving, too." I knew then it wasn't all on my son, and I stood my ground.

There were other moments when I realized I should've listened to my gut. Like the Suzuki violin lessons I insisted Gilli stick with. He started at two and a half—because he was bright, because I thought he could excel, and because I wanted him to. But he didn't like it. I kept telling his teachers I didn't think it was working. They said keep at it. And I did—too long. Now, he has no interest in music. He probably could've been good at it, maybe even great, but I pushed too hard. I know that. And he knows that. And that's just something we both carry.

Looking back, I think I often confused guidance with control. I wanted to do it differently from how my parents had done it with me, but sometimes I went too far the other way. I wanted to do right by my kids. I still do. But some of those lessons I had to learn the hard way.

The Fear of Passing It On

I've always been haunted by the fear that I might pass my pain on to my kids. That somehow, just by being their mother, I would give them my sadness, my anxiety, and my trauma. I was so very sensitive about the kids being protected and having the support I wish I had that I definitely overcompensated by perseverating over their well-being. I made every trial and tribulation the kids went through into a life lesson, trying to force wisdom. I didn't want them to suffer. Rather, I wanted to protect them and alleviate any possible pain. I also demanded that they respect others, be kind to others.

At one point, I suggested that Eitan call my parents every other week, just to keep some kind of connection. But over time, I realized he wasn't calling because *he* wanted to—he was doing it to please *me*. And I had to stop forcing it. I couldn't ask him to maintain a relationship that only existed to serve someone else's narrative.

We made it clear to our boys that they could have their own relationships with my parents, their grandparents, and that our estrangement didn't have to be theirs. Gilli still visits, especially because he has a natural connection with my dad. They share interests—golf, Ohio State football, politics. When Gilli visits, he plays golf, goes to the club, and enjoys their company. I'm glad for that.

Eitan has a different experience. He's younger, and things have shifted. On one visit, he called me to say he was bored. They were in assisted living by then. He expected to go from activity to activity like they used to—but now, everything was slower. He'd say, *"They're taking a nap,"* or *"There's nothing to do."* He didn't want to go back—not because he didn't care, but because the experience no longer felt right for him then. And I respected that. More recently, Eitan, like his older brother, has been enjoying a traditional yearly trip with his grandfather to Ohio State to watch the Buckeyes play.

Breaking the Cycle

Jeff and I never spoke poorly of my parents in front of our children. I made that vow and stuck to it. But I also drew boundaries. I stopped answering the phone to make arrangements, having Gilli arrange himself, or sticking to email. I stopped pretending that their behavior didn't affect me. And I stopped offering my children up to keep the peace. I broke the cycle by refusing to pretend any-more. And by giving my kids what I never had: the freedom to express how they really feel.

I created a home where there was laughter, noise, questions, and forgiveness. Where it was okay to mess up and come back together. Where being seen wasn't earned through performance but granted as a birthright.

Sometimes I still doubt myself. I still wonder if I've done enough. But when I hear my kids say *"I love you"* with ease, or when they come to me with their feelings instead of hid-ing them—I know I've already changed the story.

I wasn't raised to believe I could do this. But I'm doing it anyway. And that, more than anything, is the legacy I want to leave behind.

Lynn, My Longtime Friend

I met Karen around the time she and Jeff were adopting Gilli—so more than twenty years ago now. We both belonged to Congregation Beth Shalom, and I was working there in some capacity. I remember how naturally we connected. At some point, Karen and Jeff needed to go downtown for a night or two, and I offered to babysit Gilli. He was just a baby—not even a toddler—and I ended up being his first babysitter. I think Karen and Jeff felt comfortable leaving him with me because I already had older children. I was a single mom at the time.

That's when the friendship started. Years later, around 2005, I went to work at Federation and ended up reporting directly to Karen and Alan. Even after I moved to St. Louis in 2007, Karen and I remained close. Over the years, the boys played soccer, and they'd stay at my apartment in University City whenever their matches brought them here. If they stayed in a hotel, I'd still show up to watch them play and catch up with Karen. And I'd go to Kansas City every so often to visit friends—including Karen. Sometimes she'd come visit me too and stay a few days. We've just always stayed in each other's lives.

I first became aware of Karen's mental health struggles when she told me—very candidly—that one of the reasons she and Jeff adopted was because of her mental health history. She told me she was committed to adopting boys only, and while I never asked why, it stood out to me.

I never saw anything particularly alarming during the time we lived in the same city. It wasn't until after I moved to St. Louis that I became more aware of how difficult things had become for her. There were two periods that stood out most. The first was subtle—I would reach out, and I wouldn't hear back. Weeks might pass. I'd start to worry and text our mutual friend Ronit to ask if she had heard from Karen. She often hadn't, and we'd go back and forth, checking in with each other, trying to piece together what was going on.

12

~~~~~~~~

THE YEARS OF DARKNESS
(2019-2021) A.K.A THE BLACK HOLE

GILLI'S BAR MITZVAH (A Jewish ritual marking adulthood) was April 4, 2019. I held on for that milestone. I smiled through the pictures, showed up for brunch, and was the perfect hostess, outgoing and active. But I knew—deep in my bones—I was on the edge. Just like my body had used OCD as a crutch to survive childhood, I managed to hold it together long enough to get through the planning and the event itself. I'm not sure if it was faith or just the way my body copes—but I was able to stay *on* and create an experience that Gilli would remember in a positive light, something others could enjoy with him. I held it together because there was no other option. But I knew how painful it was to live that way—functioning on the outside while slowly dying on the inside.

And then at the end of that celebratory weekend, I stopped functioning.

That's not a metaphor. I *stopped* functioning. I couldn't get out of bed. Couldn't shower. Couldn't eat unless someone put a plate in front of me. I lived in bed with the lights off and *Law & Order SVU* playing on an endless loop. The predictability of the episodes—the rhythm of crime, investigation, justice—was the only thing that made sense. My life had become unrecognizable, but *SVU* stayed the same.

I became obsessed with homelessness. I was convinced I was going to end up on the streets. I stopped showering—not out of defiance, but because in my mind, I was preparing for the shelter. I planned it out, where I would go, what I'd pack. I wasn't suicidal in the traditional sense. I just didn't care if I lived or died. I stopped going to therapy. I avoided my kids. I lied to Jeff. I told him I'd walked the dogs, fed the kids, and taken a shower. None of it was true. I would crawl on the floor to get water because I was too weak to stand. I fainted once and hit my head. Tore an artery in my neck. I didn't even care.

Jeff tried everything. He begged. He reasoned. He threatened. He cried. Nothing worked. I was gone. And he was alone—trying to parent two children, hold down a job, and care for a wife who had mentally left the building.

There's an entire year of my life that I can't account for. A black hole. I know people visited. I know there were doctor's appointments and electroconvulsive therapy (ECT) treatments, typically used as the last resort for those who have been through medication, therapy, and other options for major depressive disorder when nothing has worked, and outpatient programs. I know Francie and Jay, Jeff's mom and dad, came to Kansas City. I know I spent Thanksgiving with Jeff's Aunt Sheila. But I wasn't *there*. My body was present, but I wasn't. I felt like an empty shell—I remember the feeling vividly. We took a family photo that day, all of us in white shirts and jeans, posed by the tree.

Then came the phone call that changed everything. In 2021, Jeff sat on the bed with me and made me talk to a psychiatrist, Dr. Z. I didn't want to talk. I didn't believe anything would help. But he asked different questions. He didn't treat me like a broken thing. He listened. Really listened. And then he said something simple and revolutionary: *"Let's figure this out together."*

He put me back on the MAOI inhibitor—the one medication that had worked for me in the past, the one everyone else had dismissed as too old school or risky. Within weeks, the fog began to lift.

I remember the first time I showered again. Not because I was told to. Not because someone begged me. But because I *wanted* to. I remember going to Eitan's soccer game and cheering. I remember picking him up from school and waving to the other parents. These might sound like ordinary things. But for me, they were miracles.

For the first time in years, I was taking naps because I was tired from activity—not because I couldn't escape the weight of my mind. My brain was working again. The chemicals were aligned. It wasn't just the medication. It was the medication, the talk therapy, and the tiniest ember of desire that had somehow, miraculously, stayed alive inside me.

I missed the entire pandemic. While the world was melting down, I was already gone. But when I came back—truly back—it was with a new understanding. Mental illness doesn't always look like sadness. Sometimes it looks like silence. Stillness. Watching reruns for twelve hours a day while the world moves on without you.

I tell this story now because someone else needs to hear it. Someone who's lying in bed, unable to shower, convinced they're just lazy or broken. You're not. You're sick. And there is help. But it has to be the *right* help. The right listener. The right treatment. The right lifeline.

Mine came in the form of a doctor who listened. A husband who wouldn't give up. And two children who needed me—even when I couldn't be there. I came back for them. And, finally, for myself.

If you're navigating depression, OCD, or any kind of mental illness—please hear me:

> *You are not alone.*

> *You are not a failure.*

> *You are not broken beyond repair.*

There were days I couldn't get out of bed. Days I couldn't hug my children. Days I believed with every cell in my body that they would be better off without me. And yet—here I am. Still their mom. Still showing up. Still healing.

It is possible to lose yourself and come back.

It is possible to parent through pain.

It is possible to repair.

You will not do it perfectly. No one does. But the moments you *do* show up matter more than the ones you miss. Your kids don't need you to be perfect. They need you to be real. To be human. To come back when you can.

Get help. Try again. And when one treatment doesn't work, try another. The right medication, the right therapist, the right *listener*—they exist. You don't have to do it all at once. You don't even have to believe fully in your recovery. You just need to stay in the room long enough for something to shift.

Your love is not erased by your illness.

Your worth is not determined by your productivity.

And your children—whether they say it out loud or not—want you.

Keep going. You're not done yet. I wasn't either.

13

BREATHING AGAIN—
A CHANGE IN THE AIR

WHEN PEOPLE TALK about recovery, they often picture it like a staircase. You move upward. You improve. You reach a higher ground. But for me, it wasn't like that at all.

It was more like standing in the middle of a dense forest after a storm. Everything around me was uprooted, scattered, damp with memory. And yet, somehow, the air had changed. I was still in the aftermath—but I could breathe again. That's where rebuilding began.

A Ripple, Not an Ocean

The shift wasn't dramatic. It didn't come with trumpets or tears. It was subtle. Quiet. Life went on. I showered. I walked the dog. I opened a window. I went to Eitan's soccer game and stood on the sidelines cheering and being present. That was it. That's how it started.

After eighteen months of being unable to function, even the smallest acts felt like rebellion against the darkness. They were not glamorous. They were not Instagrammable. But they were *mine.*

There's no ceremony for getting back out of bed after a long depression. No audience claps for brushing your teeth. No one sends flowers when you prepare a simple dinner for your children after weeks of "fend for yourself" and silence. But those were my milestones. Private victories. Proof that something inside me still worked—that there was something worth salvaging.

It felt like reclaiming fragments of myself. A smile that wasn't forced. A laugh that didn't catch in my throat. A moment with Gilli or Eitan that wasn't overshadowed by guilt or dread. Sometimes those moments lasted only a few seconds, but they were enough to remind me that I hadn't disappeared entirely.

The Right Help

Dr. Z saved my life. Not with magic. Not even with medication alone. But by *listening.* He didn't rush to label me or skim my chart like a to-do list. He asked real questions. He remembered details. He looked me in the eye and said, *"We'll figure this out."*

That meant something. It was the first time in a long time I felt like a whole person in a doctor's office—not just a diagnosis. He didn't pathologize me. He didn't patronize me. He simply held space for the real version of me—the one who had been buried under years of dissociation, fear, and shame.

He prescribed Parnate—an MAOI that had worked for me in the past but had been dismissed by other doctors as old school or risky. But it worked. Slowly, my mind returned. Thoughts became clearer. The paranoia eased. I started to hear my voice again.

Therapy helped too, but not in the "fix me" way I once imagined. It didn't solve everything, but it did give me a place to tell the truth. Therapy became my rehearsal space for the world. I could cry, rage, remember, and still walk out knowing I was held and believed.

It was also about community. My healing wasn't just supported by professionals—it was upheld by people who never stopped believing in me. Jeff, who held the household together through my collapse. Clergy and professionals, who gave me spiritual permission to live in my truth. Friends and family who texted even when I didn't answer. Their steady presence became the scaffolding for my reconstruction.

Reengaging with My Kids

The hardest part of coming back was facing what I had missed.

Eitan had grown taller. His voice had changed. He had new interests I didn't even know about. Gilli had matured, as firstborns often do in the wake of a parent's absence. He had become more independent—but also quieter around me.

The guilt was immense. There's a particular ache that comes with watching your children grow up while you're lying in bed, trying to convince yourself to live. I missed school events. I missed casual conversations. I missed late-night snacks in the kitchen and lazy Sunday mornings. I missed the rhythm of our life together.

But kids are resilient—and merciful. I had to earn their trust again. Not because they didn't love me, but because they needed to know I was *really* back. That they didn't have to tiptoe or wonder which version of me they'd get today.

I started showing up. Not with grand gestures, but with presence. I asked questions. I listened. I remembered details. I hugged them often. I said, *"I'm sorry."* I said, *"Thank you for loving me even when I couldn't show up."* And they did. They always had.

We talked more about emotions. About what it means to be human. I didn't pretend to be perfect. I let them see me make mistakes and apologize. I let them see what accountability looks like. We healed, slowly, together.

Redefining Recovery

I used to think recovery meant being symptom-free. That if I still had dark thoughts or bad days, I wasn't so-called better. But that's not true.

Recovery, for me, means knowing what I need and honoring that. It means recognizing a spiral before I'm lost in it. It means reaching out instead of shutting down. It means giving myself grace—again and again and again.

I learned to speak more kindly to myself. To stop measuring my worth by how productive I was or how many meals I cooked from scratch. I stopped comparing myself to other moms who seemed to have it all together. Comparison was poison, and I was finally learning to set it down.

Recovery isn't about becoming someone else. It's about returning to yourself and realizing you were always enough.

It's not linear. Some days I still feel the pull of that darkness. Some days I want to crawl back under the covers. But now I have tools. I have people. I have reasons to fight. And more than anything, I have perspective.

Self-Help and the Misunderstood Practice of Healing

For the longest time, I didn't know what people meant by self-care. The phrase would come up constantly— friends, therapists, social media—and I'd nod, pretending I understood. But the truth? I didn't. I had depression. I still worked out. I still showed up for things. I was functional. So, I figured I must already be taking care of myself.

But that wasn't it.

What I missed was the *why*. I thought self-care was some kind of grand gesture, or maybe just a trendy buzzword. Reading a book? Cooking dinner? Taking a walk? I'd been doing those things for years, but never for *me*. They were chores. Obligations. Cooking meant throwing together tuna and peas because we needed some vegetables with dinner, not because I enjoyed it. Working out was to stay in shape, not to feel better. I didn't understand that self-care wasn't a separate part of life—it was a way to live it differently.

It wasn't until after my breakdown in 2021 that the term took on real meaning. My therapist said it flatly: *"You have to do self-care."*

I remember blinking at him. *"You mean like ... yoga and reading?"* *"Yes,"* he said. I thought he was nuts. How was that going to help me? But slowly, it did.

I began to understand that self-care wasn't a luxury. It wasn't optional. It wasn't something you rewarded yourself with *after* the work was done. It was part of survival. It was an act of quiet resistance against the nonstop doing and pleasing and fixing. It was a way to reclaim tiny pieces of yourself, one breath, one page, one walk at a time.

The first time I really *got* it, I was in a yoga class. I'd gone for years—rolled out the mat, went through the poses, ignored the spiritual chatter. When they talked about still-ness and breathing into your body, I rolled my eyes. It felt vague, performative. I didn't buy it.

Then, one day, my mind went still.

Not because I forced it, not because I understood how—but because I finally let myself be quiet. For the first time, the noise stopped. No spirals. No lists. Just space. It hit me hard. *Oh,* I thought. *This is what they meant.* Not just yoga. Stillness. The absence of urgency. The feeling that I didn't need to solve everything right now. That was the beginning.

I started to look at everything differently. Making din-ner became an intentional act, not a chore. Sometimes it meant a real meal. Sometimes, it meant just making a salad or going for a walk instead, because that's what I needed more. I gave myself permission to not always push through. If the dishes stayed in the sink, so be it. If I skipped something to breathe, that was the win.

Before, I was always working. Always pushing. There was always one more thing that needed to be done, and it always came first. I didn't go to the gym because there was work to do. I didn't go outside because I hadn't finished the laundry. The idea that I could prioritize *myself* over a to-do list was foreign. I thought it was irresponsible. Lazy. Indulgent.

Now, I know better. It's discipline. It's courage. It's choos-ing to value yourself enough to stop.

Self-help, for me, is no longer about books or mantras or the right kind of green smoothie. It's about tiny choices. Slowing down. Paying attention. It's not performative. It's practical. It's not selfish. It's sanity.

It took me years to understand that taking care of myself wasn't a sign of weakness. It was the foundation I needed to survive—*and* to grow.

Living with Intention

Rebuilding a life wasn't about getting back to who I used to be. That person is gone. And maybe that's okay. Maybe she wasn't who I needed to be anyway.

Now, I live more slowly. More intentionally. I say *no* more often. I protect my energy. I invest in people who see me fully—not just the version of me they want. I don't perform as much. I don't hustle for love. I no longer confuse compliance with connection.

I know what I need to stay healthy. Morning light. Boundaries. Movement. Laughter. Meaningful conversation. Quiet time. A therapist who gets it. A rabbi who listens. And family who love me unconditionally. A husband who partners. Children who forgive.

I'm building something new—something that can hold both joy and grief, strength and fragility, presence and boundaries. Something that's real. Something that lasts.

OTHER
VOICES

Dana, My Friend

Mental illness, mental health, mental health awareness, mental health stigma ... these are just a few of the key terms we hear so much more today than even five, ten, or twenty years ago. Thank goodness, today, we can all talk about the world of mental health in a more supportive, calmer way rather than with a hushed tone or grave concern.

Over the past eighteen years, I've observed my good friend, Karen, face her ups and downs with mental health. I admit, there was a time when I had to take a step back and reflect on what my part was as a friend. The one question that kept swirling around in my head was "How can I be a good friend and feel SO helpless at the same time?" As our friendship grew and as she experienced various setbacks, the answer finally came to me.

I began to adopt a "Don't Know Mind," which, according to leadership strategist and colleague, Jim Davis, means "To go into <u>each</u> interaction and every opportunity to connect with a true openness to be curious, to learn, and to grow." For my friendship with Karen, I may not have had the answer or solution to her suffering from a mental *illness, but what I learned to do is to focus my energy on listening, empathizing, and learning more about what her world is like. Considering my innate drive and motivation is usually to move directly from problem to solution, this was not, and in some ways, still is not an easy task. My "Let's fix it" or "Let's make it easier" approach hasn't worked and ... maybe that's the mystery of mental illness. It's not an exact science. It's the creative and unknown adventure of playing with a mind. How scary is that? Yes, I am saddened that my friend's mind becomes an experiment with professionals engaging in trial and error, as well as situational solutions.*

But what keeps me open, positive, and forward thinking is ... Karen. I see the desire to have a healthy mind and a happy life, I see her openness to seek professional help, and I see a loving husband and kids who have a vision for a brighter tomorrow. Most importantly, I observe Karen working hard to find solutions that will enable her to be the best she can be every single day.

14

HONOR THY FATHER AND MOTHER

MY CHILDHOOD SYNAGOGUE, Tifereth Israel in Columbus, Ohio, was one of the few safe spaces I had growing up. When I walked through its doors, my shoulders relaxed just a bit. The nervous energy that constantly lived in my belly eased. For a few hours each week, I could let my guard down—if only slightly.

I was part of a small class of five students. After snacks, we would gather in the small chapel to learn the prayers for Shabbat and the holidays. I remember the red carpeted bimah and the Aron Kodesh (cabinet in a synagogue that holds the sacred Torah scrolls) at the center, its large wooden doors inlaid with Stars of David. The Eternal Light burned above it, and the Ten Commandments were etched in abbreviated Hebrew down each of the doors.

Nine of the Ten Commandments felt straightforward:

- "Thou shalt have no other Gods before me."

- "Thou shalt not make unto thee any graven image."

- "Thou shalt not take the name of the Lord thy God in vain."

- "Remember the sabbath day, to keep it holy."

But the fifth commandment—"Honor your father and your mother, so that your days may be long upon the land the Lord your God is giving you"—was not so simple for me, even at a very young age. It troubled me. Because I didn't feel love or safety in my relationship with my mother, and yet here was this divine rule that said I was required to honor her. How could I be a so-called good Jew when my heart resisted one of the commandments?

My parents used to take adult vacations every year, which felt like vacations for us, too. Their absence meant freedom, and we often had loving, energetic people—usually my dad's young office staff—stay with us. They had no children of their own, and they gave us the kind of attention and care I craved. I remember one night, when Bev and Ed were flying home, I looked up at the night sky through the small bathroom window and wished that the plane would crash—and that only my dad would survive. I was maybe ten. I remember the strange sense of relief that came with the thought—and the guilt. Where was the honor in that?

One of my favorite memories of Tifereth Israel was sitting next to my dad during Saturday services. He wore a large cream and brown tallit (a fringed garment worn as a prayer shawl), and I would sit to his right and play with the fringes. It was my quiet way of feeling close to him. But on the other side of my dad sat Bev. Occasionally, she would reach over and swat my hand away—as if even that small connection was too much.

Later, during my first year of teaching, my dad and I would meet monthly at synagogue for Friday evening services. Those forty-five minutes together meant everything to me. But they were all I got. There was never an invitation to come home for Shabbat dinner afterward—no warm gathering, no extended time. Just the service. Just the surface.

In my late twenties, I was married at Tifereth Israel. Surrounded by friends and family, I began to really ask myself: *How can I be a good Jew if I don't honor my parents?* At that time, Rabbi B, a warm and compassionate man, was the spiritual leader at Tifereth. He and his wife were always kind and loving toward me, sensing perhaps the disconnect between what my family presented publicly and what happened behind closed doors. Years later, during a friend's children's b'nei mitzvot, Rabbi B and I had an honest conversation—one that gave me permission to start asking what I could let go.

I continued exploring this idea of honor while living in Kansas City. Another rabbi, Rabbi C, who knew Jeff, me, and our son Gilli well, had two conversations with me that left a deep impact. One centered around how the Torah views toxic relationships. The other was more direct: *What happens if someone chooses not to have a relationship with a parent anymore?*

At the time, I wasn't ready to cut ties with Bev. But the question lingered. Therapy gave me language I didn't have before—words like *trauma* and *triggers*. Eventually, I recognized that Bev was a trigger for me. The dread, the shutdown, the self-doubt—I could trace it back to her presence in my life.

I met with a third rabbi, Rabbi G, a personal friend and teacher, and asked: *"How can I honor my mother without being triggered?"* He gave me an answer I've held onto ever since: *"As long as you are respectful when around her, send cards on special occasions, and don't speak badly of her in front of your children, you are honoring her."* That gave me a kind of spiritual permission. I began to believe that the Torah was written with nuance—that honor did not mean self-erasure. That honoring someone didn't mean enduring their harm.

Jeff and I spent a lot of time talking through what it would mean to cut ties and what it would mean for my healing. For our family. For our boys. We agreed that Gilli and Eitan could continue a relationship with Bev—as long as it was loving and appropriate. And for a time, it was.

But the moment I told Bev directly that I needed space—that I needed distance to heal—her rage exploded. I still remember the phone call. I referred to her as "Bev." She lost it. *"I am your mother!"* she screamed. *"You will address me as Mom!"*

Since that call, I haven't called her anything at all.

What I wasn't prepared for was Ed's response. *"If you don't have a relationship with your mom,"* he said, *"then I can't have a relationship with you."*

And just like that, I lost them both.

But in that loss, I gained clarity. I was not breaking a commandment—I was following a deeper truth. I was honoring myself. I was choosing healing. And maybe, in some small, sacred way, that is also honoring the commandment.

15

~~~~~~~~~~~

CHOOSING BOUNDARIES
AND SELF-PRESERVATION

Understanding Narcissistic Behavior

For most of my life, I thought if I just worked harder—if I explained better, forgave more, stayed quiet when it hurt most—then I could have the family I always wanted. I didn't know, for a long time, that I wasn't actually dealing with confusion or simple misunderstandings. I was dealing with narcissism.

Recognizing Bev's behavior for what it was didn't happen all at once. It crept in slowly, like the way sunlight reveals the full shape of a room at dawn. Patterns I once rationalized as normal snapped into sharp focus: the constant manipulation, the blame-shifting, the way love was offered like a prize to be won and then yanked away the moment I needed it most. Every kindness had a price. Every moment of closeness was later used as a weapon.

It was never about love, it was about control.

For years, I believed that if I could just be better, if I could anticipate her moods, keep the peace, not rock the boat, I could finally earn the love I craved. I spent decades trying. I kept thinking: *Maybe next time it will be different.*

It wasn't different. It never would be. Because it was never about me.

Choosing Me

There wasn't one sudden, cinematic moment when I realized I had to cut ties. It was more like a slow gathering of moments, quiet heartbreaks, impossible demands, boundaries bulldozed without hesitation. Triggers that just inflamed my PTSD.

But there was one final breaking point.

A conversation where I tried, again, to set a simple boundary, and watched, yet again, how effortlessly it was dismissed. There was no recognition. No curiosity. No pause to consider how I felt. There was only the same cold dismissal, the same twisting of my words to make me seem unreasonable.

Something inside me broke open.

I realized that no matter how carefully I spoke, no matter how many times I swallowed my own needs to "be the bigger person," it would never be enough. Loving them was costing me my peace, my self-worth, my future.

And in that moment, I chose me.

It wasn't clean. It wasn't easy. It wasn't without guilt or second-guessing. I grieved the idea of what could have been. I grieved the hope that maybe *this time* they would understand. But at the core, I knew:

Loyalty to dysfunction is not love. Obedience is not love. I didn't owe my life, my peace, or my children's safety to people who had never truly offered me theirs.

Walking away wasn't an act of cruelty. It was an act of survival.

My Dad's Complicity

The hardest part wasn't Bev. Deep down, I had long suspected the shape of her cruelty. The hardest part was accepting my dad's role.

For years, I clung to the image of him as the quiet protector, the one who maybe just didn't *know* how bad it was. I told myself he was trapped, too. That he was powerless. That if he *really knew*, he would have stepped in.

But the truth was simpler and far more painful: He knew. He saw. And he chose silence.

Silence wasn't neutrality. It was consent.

And once I allowed myself to see that clearly, it shattered the story I had been telling myself for decades. His silence, his constant rationalizing, his "it's not so bad" shrugs, they weren't accidents. They were choices. Choices he made again and again, even as I twisted myself into knots trying to win their approval.

I once said in therapy, *"It's like my dad was standing right next to me while I was drowning and kept saying, 'Just swim harder.'"*

Accepting that broke something open in me, a deep ache I had kept buried under layers of hope and excuses. Mourning the loss of a dad I never truly had was a grief unlike any other. It was mourning not just what was, but what never had been.

Allowing Myself to Grieve the Loss of Parents Who Were Never Truly There

Grieving them wasn't like grieving a death. Death is final; you don't expect the person to come back different. But with living parents, there's always that lingering temptation to hope. Maybe if you say it differently. Maybe if you wait long enough. Maybe if you just endure a little more.

Grieving my parents meant giving up that hope.

It meant accepting that the love I needed would never come in the form I deserved. It meant mourning birthdays with a lump in my throat, the holidays that felt more like performances than celebrations, the endless tightrope walk of trying to be palatable enough to avoid punishment.

There's a strange purity to grief once you stop resisting it. It hurts. It cuts deep. But it also clears a space inside you. A space where something new can grow.

I had to allow myself to sit in that grief, to honor it. I had to let the sadness flow through me without trying to tidy it up or make it look noble. I had to admit that I had been abandoned long before I ever chose to walk away. And strangely, allowing myself to grieve gave me something I had never had before:

Permission to choose a different kind of love.

The Last Call

It wasn't spontaneous. Jeff and I had gone over what we were going to say, maybe not a full rehearsal, but close enough. We knew it was going to be hard. But I also knew I couldn't keep doing it. For my mental health, I had to set a firm boundary.

We got on the call with both of them, Bev and Ed. I told them, as calmly as I could, that I could no longer have conversations with Bev. It wasn't safe for me. I remember the moment clearly. I said it directly: *"I can't keep hearing her voice."* And Bev lost it, full meltdown. But I didn't respond to the drama. I just let the boundary be the boundary.

Ed tried, as always, to find a workaround. He's always been the fixer, the one looking for a different way to keep things stitched together, even when the fabric is shredded.

But there wasn't another way this time. He didn't understand how serious I was at first. I remember calling him afterward, and he'd say, *"Oh, your mom's right here,"* and then try to hand her the phone, like he hadn't heard me. And I would have to hang up. I literally could not hear her voice. I couldn't have her energy near me. Eventually, he had to choose. And he chose Bev.

Even then, I wasn't angry. I just saw it clearly. He wasn't capable of honoring my boundary without violating it.

Finding Peace in the Decision to Step Away

Stepping away wasn't loud. It wasn't dramatic. There were no final confrontations, no scenes ripped from a movie. It was quieter than that.

It was choosing not to call back. It was choosing not to justify myself anymore. It was choosing not to reopen old wounds just because someone else demanded access to them.

In the silence that followed, there was sadness, yes, but also an immense, breathtaking relief. I stopped feeling like I was crazy for needing respect. But what I found on the other side wasn't just relief. It was freedom.

Freedom to build a life rooted in truth, not obligation. Freedom to create a family defined by kindness, trust, and mutual care, not fear and control. Freedom to live without the constant, gnawing question of what I had done wrong.

For the first time, I understood something no one had ever taught me:

Choosing myself wasn't selfish. It was a kindness.

Choosing peace wasn't betrayal. It was a reclamation.

And though the road to that peace was paved with grief, doubt, and loss, it was also paved with something stronger, something I had carried inside me all along: the quiet, unwavering belief that I was worthy of love. And that love could start with me.

A MESSAGE TO OTHERS WHO STRUGGLE

IF YOU'VE MADE it to the end of this book: Thank you. Thank you for staying with me, for sitting beside my younger self in the darkness, for witnessing the pain I tried so hard to hide for so long, and for walking with me on the long, hard, beautiful road toward healing.

There were years when I never imagined I would be well enough to write these words. Years when the pain in my mind felt unbearable. Years when I wasn't sure I would live to see my children grow up. But I'm still here. And I want you to know, if you're struggling: **Mental illness is not a personal failure**.

I believed it was, for far too long.

As a child, I thought something was wrong with me, something deep and unfixable. I was anxious, obsessive, always afraid I would do something bad or that something bad would happen. I thought I had to be perfect to be loved, and when I couldn't be perfect, I decided I wasn't lovable. That belief followed me into adulthood. I couldn't see that my mind had adapted to survive in a home that didn't feel emotionally safe. I didn't have the language for trauma. I didn't know what OCD was. I didn't know what dissociation meant. I just knew that I was tired, scared, and couldn't trust my brain.

Even after my first hospitalization, I still thought it was my fault. I thought if I could just try harder—be a better wife, a better daughter, a better mother—I could make it all go away. I thought I was failing everyone. It took years of therapy, medication, and peeling back layer after layer of internalized shame to realize: I wasn't failing. I was doing the best I could, with a brain shaped by fear, and a body carrying pain that no one ever helped me name.

Recovery didn't happen all at once. There was no single turning point. Healing, for me, looked like a slow, stubborn return to myself. It was the tiny moments, learning to sit still when the anxiety wanted me to run, letting myself cry in therapy without apologizing, allowing my children to see me vulnerable and still present. It was showing up, over and over again, even when I didn't feel like I deserved love or support.

For so long, I thought I was weak. But it turns out, it takes strength to survive when your thoughts betray you. It takes courage to ask for help when you've been taught to stay quiet. It takes resilience to keep showing up when your body wants to shut down. And it takes wisdom to know when to let go of the people who can't—or won't—meet you in your healing.

Some Relationships Must be Left Behind for Survival.

This was, without a doubt, the hardest truth I had to accept. I spent years trying to get my mother to see me. To hear me. To acknowledge what happened. To care in the way I so desperately needed her to. But she couldn't—or wouldn't. I kept opening the door, and she kept walking in and hurting me again. Eventually, I had to stop opening it.

I also had to come to terms with my dad's complicity. He didn't abuse me. But he enabled the abuse. He watched it happen. And he stayed quiet. That silence cut just as deep.

Letting go of those relationships wasn't an act of bitterness. It was an act of self-preservation. It was choosing my peace, my health, my life. And I had to grieve the loss—not just of my parents, but of the fantasy I clung to.

Healing Requires the Right Combination of Support, Treatment, and Self-Compassion.

That's something I want to say clearly to anyone reading this who is still in the thick of it: You don't have to do it alone. I didn't. I had therapists who held space for my pain without judgment. I had Jeff, who loved me through the worst parts of my illness without trying to fix me. I had my children, whose laughter, chaos, and needs forced me to stay grounded in the present. I had friends and family who sent texts when I didn't have the energy to respond. I had programs, outpatient and inpatient. I had medication that stabilized me when everything felt unlivable.

There is no one path to recovery, and no right way to heal. What matters is that you find what works for *you*. That you keep trying. That you let yourself be human.

There's one thing I remember vividly from my second hospitalization. I felt more like a problem to be managed than a person in pain. My dad walked beside me while my mother trailed ten steps behind, literally and emotionally. I wasn't anyone's daughter at that moment. I was something broken, something inconvenient. There was no warmth. No gentleness. Just a schedule, a set of pills, and the constant message that I needed to hold it together, no matter how much it hurt. I lay in that hospital bed thinking, *This is who I am now. This is all I'll ever be.*

That memory still haunts me. But it also reminds me how far I've come. Because that's not who I am now. I'm not just a diagnosis or a file in a drawer or a walking bundle of symptoms. I'm a mother. A partner. A friend. I'm a woman who lived through things that once felt un-survivable and lived to tell the truth about them.

You don't need to be perfect to be loved. You don't need to be healed to be worthy. You don't need to explain your pain to people who refuse to understand it. You are allowed to take up space. You are allowed to protect your peace. You are allowed to choose yourself.

If you're someone who loves a person with mental illness, I want to say thank you. It is not always easy to walk beside someone in pain. But your presence makes a difference. Your willingness to learn, to stay, to support without trying to fix—those things matter more than you know.

And to the professionals who've chosen this work, thank you. Thank you for seeing us as more than our diagnoses. Thank you for helping us believe we are more than what we've survived.

≈≈≈≈≈≈≈

VOICES OF LOVED ONES

THERE WERE TIMES in my life when I was barely holding on—when I couldn't see a way out, and even the people who loved me didn't always know how to reach me. Mental illness, especially when it's long and complicated, can make you feel like a burden, a mystery, or worse—an absence.

But I wasn't alone. Even when I was withdrawn or lost in my pain, people showed up. They didn't always know what to say or do, and sometimes they struggled just like I did. But they stayed. They kept calling, visiting, hoping. Some stepped back for a while, some got frustrated, but many found ways to love me anyway—through the mess, through the years, through the unknown.

I wanted to include this section in the book because their voices matter. This journey wasn't just mine. It belonged to all of us who lived through it together. I asked them: *What was it like to walk beside me? When did you first know something serious was going on? What helped you stay connected? What changed in our relationship? What have you learned about love, or boundaries, or resilience?*

What follows are their full reflections—unedited, unfiltered, and full of heart. Some of what they say surprised me. Some of it broke my heart a little. All of it made me feel more seen.

If you're someone going through your inner struggle, or walking alongside someone who is, I hope these stories help you feel less alone. I hope they show that love is not always perfect or easy—but it is powerful. And sometimes, it's enough to keep someone going.

BRIAN, MY BROTHER

I think the first time I really sensed something was off with Karen was when she came to visit me during my freshman year of college. She was still in high school, a senior, and I just remember thinking something's not right. She wasn't herself. She seemed deeply unhappy and kind of lost. At the time, I couldn't name it. I wasn't trained in mental health, and I was just a college kid. Looking back, maybe there were earlier signs, but that was the moment that stuck with me.

When Karen started going through more serious struggles, I was away at school and didn't know the full picture. Our parents didn't share everything—and I don't blame them for that. They wanted me to focus on my own life. I did come home during one of her hospitalizations, though, and visited her. After that, I tried to check in more often, calling regularly, but I was still very young. I didn't really understand what was happening.

Later on, when she transferred to Ohio State, we lived together for a while. That felt important to me. I wanted to be there, to look out for her. I carried some sense of responsibility—not in a burdensome way, but more as an older brother who cared.

There were definitely moments over the years when it was hard to stay connected—especially when she and Jeff made some choices about her medications that didn't sit well with me. Eventually, she ended up back in the hospital, and I was deeply concerned. But by then, she was an adult, with a husband. I was in Pittsburgh with young children of my own, trying to manage my own life. Still, I kept in touch. During harder periods, I'd call, even if I couldn't get through. I'd leave voicemails just to say I was thinking of her, that I loved her. It became one-sided at times, but I kept doing it.

Not because I expected anything in return. That's just not how I operate. I believe you reach out because it's the right thing to do, not because someone owes you something back. If I send a birthday card or make a call, it's not to keep score. I kept calling because I wanted Karen to know she wasn't forgotten—even when she couldn't respond.

I'm a social worker by training, so I came to understand a lot more about what she was facing. There were times *when I felt sad—for her, for myself, and especially for her kids. I grieved the idea that they might never really know the Karen I grew up with. But I never gave up trying to connect.*

Karen has always been passionate, protective, and forceful in the best way when she cares about something. She may come across as carefree or upbeat to people who only know her casually, but they wouldn't know the battles she's fought. I've known her my whole life, and I still learn new layers of her story.

This journey has shaped me, too. I've learned the importance of empathy—of not assuming people are okay just because they seem okay. I've also seen how important it is to take care of yourself when you're supporting someone else. That's something I tell people all the time: You can't show up for others if you're running on empty.

Over the years, I've let go of guilt. For a while, I felt like I got out of the family dynamics unscathed—like a survivor—but I realize now that's an illusion. We're all impacted in our own ways. You can't go back and change what you didn't know. What matters is how you show up now.

These days, when Karen's in a better place, our relationship is strong. We talk often, and even though we live in different states, we stay close. That's what matters. We grew up together, we've seen each other through a lot, and we're still here.

DANA, MY FRIEND

Mental illness, mental health, mental health awareness, mental health stigma ... these are just a few of the key terms we hear so much more today than even five, ten, or twenty years ago. Thank goodness, today, we can all talk about the world of mental health in a more supportive, calmer way rather than with a hushed tone or grave concern.

Over the past eighteen years, I've observed my good friend, Karen, face her ups and downs with mental health. I admit, there was a time when I had to take a step back and reflect on what my part was as a friend. The one question that kept swirling around in my head was "How can I be a good friend and feel SO helpless at the same time?" As our friendship grew and as she experienced various setbacks, the answer finally came to me.

I began to adopt a "Don't Know Mind," which, according to leadership strategist and colleague, Jim Davis, means "To go into each interaction and every opportunity to connect with a true openness to be curious, to learn, and to grow." For my friendship with Karen, I may not have had the answer or solution to her suffering from a mental illness, but what I learned to do is to focus my energy on listening, empathizing, and learning more about what her world is like. Considering my innate drive and motivation is usually to move directly from problem to solution, this was not, and in some ways, still is not an easy task. My "Let's fix it" or

"Let's make it easier" approach hasn't worked and ... may never help.

That's the mystery of mental illness. It's not an exact science. It's the creative and unknown adventure of playing with a mind. How scary is that? Yes, I am saddened that my friend's mind becomes an experiment with professionals, engaging in trial and error, as well as situational solutions.

What keeps me open, positive, and forward thinking is ... Karen. I see the desire to have a healthy mind and a happy life, I see her openness to seek professional help, and I see a loving husband and kids who have a vision for a brighter tomorrow. Most importantly, I observe Karen working hard to find solutions that will enable her to be the best she can be every single day.

I am honored to call Karen my friend.

RONIT, MY FRIEND SINCE COLLEGE

Karen and I met my very first week at Ohio State, in the fall of 1991. We were in the same Spanish class, but we also met separately through mutual friends—and we just clicked. She was a year ahead of me and had transferred in. From that moment on, we've remained friends through every stage: college, post-college, her relationship with Jeff, having kids, everything. I've witnessed nearly every phase of her illness, from early signs in college to some of her lowest points.

The first time I really became aware of Karen's mental health struggles was when she told me. I don't think I recognized any signs myself. I just remember during our college years, she was hospitalized. It must have been my junior year. She took some quarters off and was really in a dark place. At one point, she told me she had been suicidal and even homicidal. That shocked me, especially because this was the early '90s—people didn't talk openly about mental illness.

I remember visiting her when she moved in with one of her father's hygienists. I'd go over to her place, bring ice cream, watch movies, just try to be present. Then later, she had a period where she was living alone near her parents' house and was very suicidal. I'll never forget that apartment. That time is etched in my memory.

After college, I moved to Israel, and when I came back to Columbus, she had moved to Florida with Jeff. Not long after, she got very sick again and came back to Ohio. That's when she was hospitalized in a state facility—and that was extremely hard. I was only twenty-three at the time, working at the Jewish Community Center (JCC), living on my own. I had never been to a state institution before. It was bleak and sterile, and it confused me. Karen came from a family with means—her father was a doctor—and I couldn't understand why she wasn't in a private facility.

During those months, I visited her three times a week—sometimes on my lunch break, sometimes after work. She was heavily medicated and not always communicative. I don't even think she remembers much of that time. It was traumatic for me. I remember once a friend of hers flew in to visit and stayed with me. We went to the hospital together and ended up washing Karen's hair in the bathroom sink. That's where she was—unable to care for herself, and in a very bad state.

Through it all, I stuck by her. Karen had always been a generous, kind, loving friend, and I never forgot that. I knew that the woman I saw during those dark periods wasn't all of her. I'd seen her get better before, and I held onto that hope. I wasn't trying to fix her because I knew that wasn't my role. But I wanted her to know she wasn't alone.

Looking back, I wish I'd gotten therapy earlier. Some of it was really traumatic—especially being asked by her parents to move in with her because they were afraid she might take her own life. I was twenty-one years old. I remember calling my parents, and they were horrified. That kind of responsibility at that age ... it was overwhelming.

One of the biggest things I've learned through this friendship is that being there for someone doesn't mean they'll always be happy to see you, or even respond. When I visited Karen in the hospital, she wasn't always glad to see me. That wasn't the point. I wasn't doing it to feel better about myself—I was doing it so she wouldn't be alone. Even if she couldn't process it, I was showing up. That mattered to me.

Karen is a very intense friend—fiercely loyal, deeply emotional. There were times, years later, when she called me out because she felt disconnected from me. And she wasn't wrong. I was a single parent working full time, running non-profits, navigating a lot—but when she said it, I heard her. And I recommitted. That's just who she is—she doesn't let go of people she loves.

Today, our relationship is good. We don't talk constantly, but we're in each other's lives. She came to my kids' b'nai mitzvah, made a huge effort to show up. I've been to Kansas City for work and always made a point to see her. She embraces every day with intention now, and I think, in part, she's trying to make up for some of the time she lost when she was unwell.

If I had to give advice to someone supporting a friend with mental illness, it would be this: Get your own support. You're not supposed to solve it. Being a friend isn't the same as being a therapist. You can't fix them. But you can show up. You can bear witness. And you can do it without expecting anything in return.

Mental illness is not something that just goes away. It's like a scar—it might fade, but it never fully disappears. It becomes part of who you are. Most days, it doesn't hurt. But every once in a while, something rubs against it—a memory, a trigger, a moment of stress—and it reminds you that the pain was real. Karen has carried her scars for a long time. I've seen her fall, and I've seen her heal. And I've seen her walk through the world with strength, even when those old wounds start to sting.

I've also learned that you never really know what someone else has been through. People see Karen now—active in the community, present, vibrant—and they have no idea what it took for her to get here.

But I do.

And I'm proud to still be standing beside her.

JEFFRY, MY HUSBAND

We first met through BBYO in high school—same region, Kentucky, Indiana, and Ohio. I went to a regional meeting in Dayton, Ohio, by chance, and that's where we first connected. We were juniors. But we didn't date then; we became close friends first. Back in those days, we wrote actual letters—like with stamps—and we did that for years. We were each other's confidants. We knew everything about each other's lives—boyfriends, girlfriends, hopes, frustrations. We didn't start dating until I was in my fourth year of optometry school—nearly a decade later.

Looking back, I've thought a lot about when I first realized something was going on with Karen's mental health. It's hard to pinpoint. I remember visiting her childhood home in high school—the vacuumed carpet with the perfect lines made an impression—but I don't remember much else about her parents then. During college, we didn't see each other much. The first real time I saw something up close was in Florida.

Karen was living in Fort Lauderdale, and I was in Miami. She had a good job, a few close friends, and her grandmother was nearby, with whom she was really close. Things seemed stable. And then—suddenly—it wasn't. It was a total breakdown. I was shocked at how fast everything unraveled. At first, I tried to convince her to stay, but she was just not functioning. Her parents came to take her back to Ohio. Not long after that, she was hospitalized. That was tough. We were engaged at the time. I remember going to see her once while she was hospitalized, but contact was really limited. Honestly, I probably tried to suppress a lot of that time. It was painful for both of us.

That first engagement is kind of a funny story, though. We had dinner with her grandmother and aunt, and afterward, I tried to get her to go for a walk on the beach. She didn't want to. She was cold and annoyed. I practically dragged her onto the sand—she was full-on pissed—and in the middle of all that, I proposed. Somehow, she still said yes. We laugh about that a lot now.

We never completely disconnected after her hospitalization, but things were distant. Her parents took over—understandably, I guess—and I think they felt a strong sense of responsibility for her well-being. I was just a grad student. Still, there was this lingering feeling that they *treated her like something fragile, and I wasn't sure how to re-enter that space.*

A few years later, we got re-engaged. Same ring. Much less drama. More of a mutual decision—we were still together, she was doing better, and it felt like it was time. From that point on, I've been there through it all. There were parts of her story I wasn't present for, like her childhood, but everything since our teens—I've seen firsthand. Sometimes close up, sometimes from afar.

We've lived through the "black holes" together. That's what we call the worst episodes—Nashville, Wisconsin— those periods were like black holes. You get pulled into something chaotic, mysterious. You don't know what's happening, and when you finally come out the other side, you can't explain what just happened. It's ungraspable. The term stuck. We still use it.

Living with someone who's had breakdowns like that changes you. During those times, it was vital for me to keep some structure. Therapy has never really clicked for me— Karen's always encouraged it, but I haven't found the right person. What helped me was a physical routine. I swim early in the morning, and even when Karen was in treatment, I kept that up. I adjusted it so I could be home in time for the kids. That gave me something to hold onto, especially when everything else was out of my control.

One thing I've learned—and I say this to anyone who loves someone with mental health issues—is that there's a massive difference between everyday struggles and full-on decompensation. Most people with mental health challenges won't go through what Karen did. But when someone does—when they break down completely—it's unpredictable. It's not like a thunderstorm you can wait out. Sometimes it's a drizzle, sometimes a tornado. And you just don't know which it's going to be.

For a long time, I was hypervigilant. I'd come home from swimming and look for signs. If the lights weren't on, I'd panic. I'd assume something was wrong. I'd ask her constantly, "Are you okay?" That's not sustainable—for either of us. I had to learn to stop looking for clues in every little thing. Now, if she says she's not feeling well, I ask, "Physical or emotional?" If it's emotional, I ask, "Should I be concerned?" And most of the time, it's just a bad day. That shift in perspective made a big difference. I had to stop living in the shadow of the last crisis.

And I think that helped our relationship, too. Karen didn't need me constantly hovering. No one wants to feel like they're under surveillance. Once I backed off, we had more room to actually live—not just brace for the next collapse.

Karen's stronger than most people know. From the outside, people see someone who gets stuff done—because she does. But they don't see the work she puts into staying well. Daily yoga, therapy, mindfulness—none of that is accidental. She's worked as hard on herself as she has on anything else in her life. And she's fiercely committed to helping others, too. This book is a part of that. It's her way of being loud about something most people are quiet about.

HARRIETTE, MY TEACHER AND FRIEND

I first met Karen when she was a freshman in high school. I was her speech teacher that year, and I had a one-year-old at home. We were in the middle of moving to a new place, and I asked Karen if she babysat. She said yes. That very same day—our chaotic moving day—I brought her over, and she ended up having to take my baby to my parents' house, put him to bed, and handle the whole evening. She did it all with such ease and maturity. After that, she became our regular babysitter every weekend. Over time, we grew very close.

Karen had a strong group of friends in high school through BBYO and camp. She seemed steady, grounded, and joyful during that period. I didn't realize the extent of her difficulties at home until much later. Her mom always struck me as very strict and someone hard to communicate with. But Karen never showed any signs that something was seriously wrong, not in high school. She was always warm, responsible, and fun to be around. Our house was full of laughter when she and her friends came over.

It wasn't until college that I began to notice shifts. She went away to Stephens College, and I'm still not exactly sure what happened there as she didn't talk much about it. Later, she was at Ohio State, and I learned that her parents wouldn't let her come back home. That's when I told her she could stay with us—as we had a spare bedroom, and my husband was setting up a business out of town. It seemed like a good situation, and I trusted her completely. Even then, though, I didn't recognize the deeper struggles she was facing.

There were hints. She would say things like, "I'm not sure about my sexuality," or "I feel uncertain about who I am." But I was juggling young kids, teaching, and a big move—it was easy to chalk it up to typical college uncertainty. She was so good at keeping up a brave front, at seeming fine.

Looking back, I realize she never really confided in me until years later. I think she wanted to preserve a certain image—maybe because I'd been her teacher, maybe because I always told her how much I admired her life and her friendships. I truly did. I used to say, "I hope my kids grow up to have what you have." But I see now that there was a lot I didn't understand.

We drifted for a while. I invited her to my son's Bar Mitzvah, and when she didn't come, I was hurt. She'd known him since he was one. I couldn't understand it at the time. Only later did she explain she'd been in a very dark place then. That was the beginning of her opening up more.

She eventually told me about the pain of her relationship with her parents—how unsupported she felt, how her father simply went along with her mother. I also learned more about her mental health once she had married Jeff and moved to Kansas City. It made sense of things—moments I'd misunderstood as her pulling away, when really, she was overwhelmed and hurting.

Her struggles absolutely affected our relationship. Not knowing the truth made me take things personally. Once I understood, my entire perspective shifted. I stopped seeing it as something about me and started understanding what she had been carrying. I also realized her mother had disliked me—openly, actually—and I never knew why. In hindsight, I think it was because of how close I was with Karen. Her mother may have resented that Karen had a positive adult connection outside the home.

When Karen eventually shared more of her story—what she'd been through, how she'd gotten help, what the right medications and support system had done for her—I felt relieved. The Karen I had known and loved was still there. My whole family loves her. My mother loves her. She was part of our family. She still feels like an older daughter or sister to my kids, because she helped raise them. They could be silly with her, rely on her. That bond never really broke.

What I wish people knew about Karen is how much is always swirling in her mind. When she talks a lot, it's not because she's scattered or overcommunicating—it's because she needs to talk it through to make sense of what's going on inside. She is incredibly kind and would do anything for someone she loves, but there are roadblocks inside her that make it hard for that generosity to always come through. Getting the right treatment has helped her so much—those blockages have lessened, and the caring, grounded Karen has reemerged more fully.

I'm a big believer in the power of medication and the right therapy. I've seen how much of a difference it's made for her—not just in how she relates to others, but in how she sees herself.

And I have to say—Karen is one of the strongest people I know. The strength it takes to face what she's faced, to raise children while navigating mental health challenges, to show up again and again even after setbacks—that's not ordinary. That's resilience. And I truly believe she doesn't even realize how strong she is. I think she underestimates it sometimes. But from where I stand, it's clear: She has a strength that's absolutely remarkable and that I respect.

SHIRLEY (AUNT SHUSH), MY AUNT

I am Karen's Aunt. I'm the sister of her father and I've been close to Karen, Malinda, and Brian since they were little. Of course, everyone calls me 'Aunt Shush,' and I love that.

From early on, I noticed something in Karen that felt familiar. We shared a kind of quietness, a tendency to step back from the crowd. When all the cousins gathered—nine kids under one roof during the holidays—she sometimes hung back, just like I used to. Maybe it was childhood resentment or simply our personalities, but in that, we became kindred spirits. I always felt a special bond with her.

Even during the hardest periods of her life, especially when she was hospitalized, I stayed in touch. Whenever she felt up to it, she'd come to the phone. And when she couldn't, I still remained her link to my mother—her grandmother. I never stopped being present. I was there to listen without judgment, to remind her she was loved. She called those times "the black hole," and I understand why, because it felt like that—like something was swallowing her up. But I never stopped believing she'd find her way out.

At one point, she came to live with us after her stay in Columbus. She didn't feel safe or comfortable at home, and we welcomed her without hesitation. We made one request—that she keep going to therapy—and she did. Within a few months, she felt strong enough to get a job and move forward on her own. It wasn't six months as I'd thought—it was probably closer to three or four—but it was her choice to take that next step. We were just there behind her, like we would be for our own children.

To me, Karen has always been the same person: sensitive, caring, and deeply moral. Even when she wasn't stable, even in the worst of it, I never lost faith in her strength. She's resilient. Today, I see someone who is happy, vital, and vibrant. I admire who she is and the life she's built. She still *carries that sensitivity, but she also shows people her best, even when it's hard for her.*

If I were to offer advice to others walking beside someone who struggles with mental health, it would be this: offer uncontested love. Just be one step behind, as my husband always said about our kids. Be close enough so they can turn and reach for you when they need to. That's what I tried to do for Karen—and what she, in turn, offers so many others now.

RON AND EILEEN, MY FAMILY IN FLORIDA, COUSINS

Ron:

Karen's father, Ed, is my first cousin. We grew up together in the same house in Cleveland, Ohio, when we were kids. As adults, though, we lost touch. I moved to Florida with Eileen in our twenties, and he made his life in Columbus. Other than the occasional family update, we weren't really in contact—until Karen called out of the blue.

She was thinking about relocating to Florida and wanted to understand the Jewish community down here— Federation, JCC, that sort of thing. At the time, I was active on the board of Federation and very involved in Jewish philanthropy. Karen and I didn't really know each other, but one conversation led to another, and before we knew it, she came to stay with us while she got settled.

Eileen:

It's funny because she initially wanted to speak with me about Jewish organizations, even though Ron was the one heavily involved, not me. Still, we immediately formed a bond. She stayed in our home, and even though we hadn't known each other beforehand, it felt natural. We became close—like surrogate parents, or an aunt and uncle. She was part of our lives here in Florida.

Eventually, she got her own apartment with a roommate we helped connect her with. But it didn't work out too well—the roommate was usually away at her boyfriend's, and Karen spent a lot of time alone. Over time, we started to notice signs that she was struggling. She shared with us that she had mental health issues and was on medication. For a while, she seemed stable, but then there was a clear downturn.

Ron:

I got in touch with her father, and eventually, Karen was hospitalized. I can't recall exactly where or when, but I do remember that she wasn't doing well. Later on, Jeff came down to Florida for his fellowship at Bascom Palmer Eye Institute, and we maintained our connection with both of them. Even when they moved to Kansas City, we stayed in touch.

Eileen:

I'll never forget when Karen asked me and Jeff's mother to go wedding dress shopping with her. Not her mother—us.

That said a lot about the kind of connection we had, and about her relationship with her mom. I felt for her. I think her mother was very controlling. I don't know all the details, but I could see that they just didn't have that mother-daughter bond.

Ron:

Karen was like family to us. She confided in us. We listened. We cared. Even when she moved away, we'd stop through Kansas City on road trips and grab a meal with her and Jeff. I remember a time when she and the boys came back from a cruise and stayed with us. She went straight to bed and barely got up. She was clearly in the midst of another episode. Her youngest must've been around seven. I took the boys out. We did our best to make them feel safe.

Eileen:

That visit broke my heart. She was in so much pain. I didn't know what to do except be there. Love her. Hug her. Make sure the boys were okay. We were in touch with Jeff the whole time, but it's hard to know what to do in those moments. When someone you love is in crisis, and you're not a professional, all you can offer is your presence.

Ron:

Our philosophy was: We're here, we love her, and if something serious is happening, we make sure the right people—Jeff, her dad—know. We weren't trying to fix anything we weren't qualified to fix. But we were always there to be a safe place.

Eileen:

If I had any advice for others supporting someone with mental illness, it would be: Listen, don't judge, offer your love. And get help from professionals when needed. My mother struggled with mental illness, so I had some sense of the ups and downs. I knew how isolating and frightening it can be—for everyone involved.

Ron:

And we'd add: don't underestimate the value of just being present. You might not be able to fix anything, but your care matters. Sometimes, that's what gets someone through.

Eileen:

Karen is so bright, loving, and insightful. She's a special person. That's obvious to anyone who spends even a little time with her. She's been through a lot, but she's open, warm, and deeply thoughtful.

Ron:

We're honored to have been part of her life. We met her in her early twenties, and she's been in our hearts ever since. It's truly been a mitzvah to know her.

Eileen:

And we're proud of her. Proud that she's telling her story, trying to help others. That takes courage.

EITAN, MY SON

I'm Eitan, my mom's youngest son. I'm fifteen now, but the first time I realized something serious was going on with my mom, I was probably in third or fourth grade. I don't remember the exact moment—it just kind of crept in. She was in bed a lot, more than usual. And she wasn't really around like she used to be. I'd get up and maybe she'd take me to school, but that didn't happen often. I'd come home and sort of figure out my day on my own. Sometimes my dad was around, sometimes not, depending on work. But mostly, she was in bed. And I really didn't have much help with stuff.

At the time, I didn't fully understand what was happening. I'd check in on her, ask if she needed water or anything. But I didn't get that it was mental illness. I didn't know what depression was. I just knew my mom wasn't there in the way she had been before, and that was really hard.

It wasn't until a few years later, after I started going to therapy and talking to people about it, that I began to understand. I realized that what my mom was going through wasn't the kind of illness where you're going to die, but something deeper—mental illness. I still struggle with anxiety myself, and I think part of it came from that time. But having the words to explain it made a difference.

It was definitely a struggle not having my mom in the way I needed her. That missing piece was huge. But things started to get better. It was a process—there were different medications—but eventually, the doctors found something that worked, and now she's doing amazing.

Our relationship is way better now. Like, 100 percent better. We actually hang out. Just the other night, we went to see the new live-action Lilo & Stitch movie together. She loved it. I feel like I can really spend time with her now, and the more I grow and learn about what she went through, the more I appreciate her.

People might not see it; my mom is one of the hardest-working people I know. She volunteers constantly and is writing this book. She does a lot.

If I had advice for another kid whose parent is going through depression, I'd say: Stay strong. Try to take time to understand what's going on, because it helps to know how to handle it. If I'd had more understanding early on, it probably would've made a big difference for me. And talk to someone—therapy helped. Even if you don't know exactly what to do, just being there for them matters.

LYNN, MY LONGTIME FRIEND

I met Karen around the time she and Jeff were adopting Gilli—so more than twenty years ago now. We both belonged to Congregation Beth Shalom, and I was working there in some capacity. I remember how naturally we connected.

At some point, Karen and Jeff needed to go downtown for a night or two, and I offered to babysit Gilli. He was just a baby—not even a toddler—and I ended up being his first babysitter. I think Karen and Jeff felt comfortable leaving him with me because I already had older children. I was a single mom at the time.

That's when the friendship started. Years later, around 2005, I went to work at Federation and ended up reporting directly to Karen and Alan. Even after I moved to St. Louis in 2007, Karen and I remained close. Over the years, the boys played soccer, and they'd stay at my apartment in University City whenever their matches brought them here. If they stayed in a hotel, I'd still show up to watch them play and catch up with Karen. And I'd go to Kansas City every so often to visit friends—including Karen. Sometimes she'd come visit me too and stay a few days. We've just always stayed in each other's lives.

I first became aware of Karen's mental health struggles when she told me—very candidly—that one of the reasons she and Jeff adopted was because of her mental health history. She told me she was committed to adopting boys only, and while I never asked why, it stood out to me.

I never saw anything particularly alarming during the time we lived in the same city. It wasn't until after I moved to St. Louis that I became more aware of how difficult things had become for her. There were two periods that stood out most. The first was subtle—I would reach out, and I wouldn't hear back. Weeks might pass. I'd start to worry and text our mutual friend Ronit to ask if she had heard from Karen. She often hadn't, and we'd go back and forth, checking in with each other, trying to piece together what was going on.

The second—and scariest—was during the pandemic. Karen became unreachable again, and after multiple attempts to connect, I finally reached out to her brother Brian. I had never involved him before, but I didn't have Jeff's contact information, and I was truly worried. I asked her brother Brian if he could get in touch with Jeff for me, and he did. Jeff told me Karen was really struggling, spending most of her time in bed, and barely functioning. He said, "Keep doing what you're doing," so I kept calling, kept texting, just trying to reach her in any way.

Eventually, she responded. She told me she'd been very ill, and that she was starting to feel better—but it had been a whole year. It was hard. I remember how transparent she was when we did reconnect. She told me she hadn't been able to be there for her kids or Jeff. She was doing EMDR therapy, which she said helped a lot. But hearing how sick she'd been—that was a wake-up call.

During that time, I remember noticing that Karen hadn't cut her hair, which was unusual for her. I later realized it was probably because she hadn't had the energy to care for herself in that way. Her physical appearance changed too—sometimes she was very thin, other times more herself. It was clear to me that her illness took a real toll.

But none of that changed our friendship. I've struggled with depression myself. I take medication. I've called up my therapist when I need a tune-up session. So, I understood, at least a little. I never judged her, and I never felt differently about her because of it.

In fact, we've supported each other over the years. We've remained loyal to each other—checking in, showing up in the ways we can, even from different cities. I remember a visit during the pandemic when she and Eitan came to stay. We were sitting at my Shabbat table, just the two of us, and she seemed really hyper—maybe from stress, maybe from what she was going through. She shared how hard things were at the time, especially with Eitan struggling and the school not being helpful. But even then, she was present. She talked. She cared. She was trying.

Professionally, Karen was always impressive. When I worked under her at Federation, she was a superstar. I had no clue she was struggling with mental health issues at that time. If she was, she hid it well—or she was in a good place. I admired her drive, her commitment, and how she went on to get her executive MPA. She's always been someone who gives her all.

She never told me she was writing a book—until she sent the email recently. When I saw her last week, she casually mentioned our interview, and I was surprised. But I think it's incredibly brave. There's still such a stigma around mental illness, and maybe—just maybe—the pandemic started to chip away at that. I hope this book helps keep chipping.

If I had advice for anyone supporting a loved one through mental illness, it would be this: Don't give up. Be there. Listen. Don't try to fix them. Just show up however you can. People don't always get better. Some do. Some come back from the depths. But being present—without judgment, without advice—is the most powerful gift you can give.

Karen is one of the most honest, loyal, empathetic people I know. She's a fierce advocate for herself and her boys. She's deeply committed to Judaism and Israel. She's also incredibly smart and has a great laugh. Some people may have seen her during her lowest points and not understood the why. But I know the why. And I love her just the same.

She's one of the bravest people I know.

GILLI: MY SON

I'm Gilli, Karen Gerson's oldest son.

To be honest, I don't really remember a clear first moment when I realized something was wrong with my mom's mental health. I just have scattered memories from that time as it was a long time ago, and I was pretty young. But I knew something was off, even if I didn't understand what it was.

From seventh grade through the middle of high school, things at home were very different. My mom spent most of her time in her room. When I got home from school, I'd be on my own. If my dad wasn't home from work, I basically had free rein. Looking back, I realize there was a real lack of parenting, but at the time, I just thought, Cool, I can do whatever I want.

During COVID, things didn't feel too different in that regard. I was home all day on Zoom school, stuck in my room doing class after class. After school, it was the same— no parental presence unless my dad was around. And back then, I wasn't very into school, so the lack of supervision gave me more freedom than I probably should have had. It felt great in the moment, but in hindsight, I think I could've used more structure during those years.

I rarely saw my mom during that time. She was just… in her room. I didn't really know what to make of it, and no one told me the full story. I think I've mentally blocked out a lot of that time. Even now, I'm not sure I ever got the full picture.

When she got better—when they found the right medication—it was like a light switch flipped. Suddenly, she was present again, back in my life. It was honestly confusing. I had spent four years figuring out how to take care of myself, how to structure my day, how to be independent—and then suddenly, I had a parent again, someone stepping in and trying to be involved. It felt like a stranger was trying to parent me. Not in a mean way—just in a jarring, disorienting way.

However, I was happy to have her back, and we have a good relationship now. I love her and I can remember all the memories from when I was younger. But the emotional shift was massive. Nobody around me seemed to acknowledge what had happened. It was like the past four years didn't exist to them, but they did for me. I had changed a lot in that time, and it felt like my mom had missed all of it.

I think some distance is inevitable when someone is gone—emotionally or physically—during such crucial years. When I'm upset or dealing with something personal, I tend to turn to my friends rather than my parents. That's just how I adapted.

I've been through multiple friend groups over the years. My social world shifted a lot—between switching schools, changing soccer teams, and eventually moving toward college. But my coping strategy during those tougher years was pretty simple: I just got out of the house. Hanging out with friends was a way to escape.

Even after learning it was depression, I didn't blame my mom. I never thought she didn't want to be there for us as it was clear something was blocking her from being able to. Knowing the name of it—"severe depression"—didn't change much for me emotionally. I had already come to terms with the fact that it was something outside her control.

If I had to give advice to someone else going through something like this, I'd say: Take care of yourself. As much as you want to fix it or understand it, you won't be able to.

What you can do is focus on your own mental and physical well-being. It's not your fault. Blaming yourself is only going to make things harder, and it won't help anyone.

My relationship with my mom now is solid. We talk often—every other day when I'm at school. Every Friday night, she calls to give me the Shabbat blessing. We've taken trips together, too. One of the most meaningful was when we went to Israel in late 2023 to volunteer after the October 7 attacks. That trip was actually her idea. She called me one day and said she felt drawn to go, and she asked if I wanted to come. I said yes immediately.

That trip changed everything for me. Being there, volunteering, and seeing the country in that context made me realize that I wanted to be there longer-term. I told my mom during that trip that I was thinking about joining the Garin Tzabar program and eventually the Israel Defense Forces. She supported me completely. As soon as we got home, I started the application process, and now I'm in the final stages of getting everything approved. That trip brought us closer.

ELISA, MY LONGTIME FRIEND

I have known Karen—whom I lovingly call 'Bonehead'—since we first met in 1984 during our summers at Camp Ramah in Conover, Wisconsin. She calls me Bonehead, too. We were bunkmates. From the beginning, Karen was kind, vibrant, effortlessly put together, and magnetic—everyone loved her. She arrived each summer with a fresh, stylish haircut and an air of quiet confidence. I've always adored her deep, sultry voice; it still makes me smile.

I grew up in Overland Park, Kansas, so when I heard that Bonehead was moving there, I was excited—and, if I'm honest, a little envious. Not because I didn't want her in my town, but because it felt like she was stepping into my past life—sending her kids to the same school I attended from kindergarten through twelfth grade and befriending many people I had grown up with. It was a strange but beautiful overlap.

When I first learned that Bonehead was struggling with her mental health, I reached out immediately. She's my dear friend, but it was also deeply personal as I had my hidden history with mental illness. My mother was both mentally and physically ill for most of my life, and camp had been my sanctuary, too. It was where I felt the most me.

I never talked about it back then, but I can now: I carried shame, sadness, and embarrassment about my upbringing. My brother also lives with mental illness. So, I understood on some level. I knew I wanted to show up for Bonehead in a way that said, "You are not alone."

Even when we weren't in constant contact, I stayed present through texts and voice messages—telling her that I loved her, that I was here, that she didn't need to respond.

I tried to be a steady presence. I stayed lightly in touch with Jeffry and a few Kansas City friends who had glimpses into her situation. I was at both brises for her boys, made an effort to connect whenever I visited town, and attended Gili's bar mitzvah.

When Bonehead was doing well, our friendship picked up just as it had when we were twelve and thirteen, like no time had passed. But there were definitely times when we were more in touch than others. I wish I had been more present during certain stretches, especially when I didn't fully understand what was going on. I knew she was depressed, but not the full scope until more recently. Even then, I never questioned staying connected—I just tried to keep reaching out with love and patience.

Our friendship has only deepened. Karen has also been an incredible support to me, especially when I needed guidance for helping others close to me who live with mental illness. The more I learn about her journey, the more in awe I am. I try to tell her that as often as I can.

Karen—Bonehead—is one of the strongest people I've ever known. She's also one of the most fiercely loyal. She would do anything for the people she truly loves.

JENNY, MY FRIEND

I first met Karen about twenty years ago. My son Cole was six months old, and Karen had just adopted Gilli. We met at Gymboree—a little music and play program for babies. From the very beginning, I was drawn to her energy. She was vibrant, happy, and just seemed like a wonderful mom. That's honestly what made me want to be her friend. She seemed so joyful in her role as a mother, and I remember thinking how Gilli looked just like her—it blew my mind when she told me he was adopted.

In those early years, Karen didn't show any signs of struggling with her mental health. If anything, she seemed to be in a really good place. We spent a lot of time together, especially as our boys had playdates, and later, we even started running together. When you run, you talk a lot—you really get to know someone. Over time, Karen started opening up about her upbringing and her struggles, especially around her relationship with her mom. That's something we really bonded over. We had similar experiences.

The first time I realized something was wrong was around 2018 or 2019. I hadn't heard from her in a while, which was unusual. When I finally saw her again, she told me what was going on—and I could see it. She didn't look like herself. It wasn't just physical—it was everything. She wasn't the same Karen I had first met. Something had changed, and I could tell she was really struggling.

That time definitely affected our relationship. She started to pull away from people. And honestly, I didn't know what to do. When someone you care about is in pain, and you don't know how to help, it's hard. But I'm a loyal person, and I believe in being there through the ups and downs. I never gave up on her. Even when she distanced herself, I gave her space—but I didn't disappear. I stayed connected in the ways I could, and when she was ready, I was there.

When she started to come out of that dark period, it wasn't like flipping a switch. It was slow. She once told me, "I had to put in the work," and I really respected that. Watching her rebuild herself was like watching someone recover from something like cancer—you can see the toll it takes, but also the strength it takes to heal. That's what Karen did. She put in the work to get better.

What helped me stay close was just listening—trying to put myself in her shoes. I know she didn't have a lot of support from her parents, and that's something I think people might not understand. It's easy to judge when someone decides to cut off a parent, but in Karen's case, I see it as an act of self-preservation. She took control of her story and made the hard decisions that were best for her mental health. That took courage.

Karen is one of the most genuinely good people I know. We're not of the same faith, but she's always so sweet about things like Christmas lights—she loves people. She loves joy.

I don't think she got the mom she needed growing up, but I really believe she's become the kind of mom she always wished she had. She's incredibly loving and committed to her children.

If I had to give advice to someone who has a friend going through depression, I'd say: Keep your head above water and just stay. Be present. You might not know exactly how to help, but your presence matters. Sometimes people in that state don't realize how deeply others care or how worried we are. Just knowing they're loved and supported can mean everything.

Karen has a lot to offer the world. I'm proud of the journey she's taken, and I hope she continues to share her story—because I know it will help people.

ACKNOWLEDGMENTS

IT WAS DRILLED into me at a very early age that, at the end of the day, your siblings are all you have. My early life was enriched by my first and closest friend—my hero in many ways—my brother Brian. As we've grown older, our bond has only deepened, and he, along with his entire family, continues to bring so much joy and strength into my life. My sister Malinda embodies resilience and strength, and I'm grateful that we've been able to raise our families in the same city. My luck is that her son and daughter are here, so I have the privilege of watching them grow up and being involved in their experiences.

I am appreciative to Ed and Bev for investing in my Jewish identity—sending me to Camp Ramah, where I first experienced living Jewishly twenty-four-seven, and giving me the opportunity to participate in BBYO at the chapter and regional levels. Their love and traditions of Ohio State are part of mine and my family's traditions, especially when it comes to football.

To Grandma Goldie—my confidante, cheerleader, and role model—thank you for showing me what it means to live life to the fullest, even in the face of obstacles. I was fortunate to have a few years with her in my 20's and truly learned what matters most in life—how important dignity and laughter are to living fully.

My Aunt Shush (who I call Tushie Shushie), my second mom, and Uncle Neal took me in when I had nowhere else to go and loved and natured me back to health. My Aunt Shush is the most loving and nonjudgemental person I've ever known—and she is often the first person I call when life throws something big my way.

The luckiest day was when I met Jeffry. We became pen pals—real letters, not emails—and saw each other at BBYO events and on visits to Chicago. In our twenties, we married. He has seen me at my best and stood by me through my worst, always showing up.

Our first son, Gilli, has challenged and inspired me since he was two. Watching him mature has taught me the power of self-confidence, perseverance, and boldly experiencing life. Gilli is true to himself—a lesson that takes most people years to understand, yet my son models it for me daily.

Eitan, our baby, has been full of joy and silliness since the day he was born. He is one of the strongest young people I know, who has faced his challenges head-on with humor, strength, and grace. Eitan's strength and "got to" attitude have been invaluable on the harder days. You can not find a young person anymore determined to overcome obstacles and prove his worth than this bright, funny and capable young man—who I am lucky enough to call my son.

Over the course of my life, I've been fortunate to have women step into mothering roles for me when I needed it most—when I didn't feel mothered in the ways I longed for. My first camp counselor at the JCC day camp, my beloved kindergarten teacher at Cassingham Elementary, and my patient, warm tutor, who offered quiet strength and confidence at her kitchen table. At Bexley High School, Harriette Kraus, my speech and English teacher, modeled what a healthy mother's relationship looks like. She became a lifelong mentor and eventually welcomed me into her family. Her kids have been part of my life since they were toddlers. When I moved to Florida for a teaching job, I struck gold— Ronnie and Eileen took me in as their own and treated me like a daughter. They were there for the worst of times and keep showing up! They remain a grounding force in my life. Even if we don't talk often, I know that if I ever need anything—or simply a smile through the phone—they will always be there.

During college, I was embraced by the family of my first love. His mother, Marilynn, also treated me like a daughter in a house full of sons. And when I met Jeff, I also gained his wonderful family—Francie, Jay, and Shane (and later on Samara). Francie has shown me unconditional love for over forty years, standing by me through every high and low.

Here in Kansas City, Lisa Cohen (and her husband Lenny) has been a true second mom—supporting not only me but my entire family, especially through the darkest periods of my illness. These women—whether still with us or remembered in love—never asked me to prove anything. I didn't have to earn their love. I just had to show up. Even when I couldn't see the real me, they held onto her until I could find my way back. Their belief in me has never wavered, and I carry each of them with me, always.

I'm incredibly grateful to the many friends and family, some of whom read early drafts of this book, who were willing to be interviewed and share their own experiences of loving me. Their honesty and vulnerability helped shape this story into something I hope can serve others. My lifelong camp friends—Suzy Frisch, Raliegh Johnson, Elisa Heligman-Recht, and Shira Shiloah—have been by my side for over thirty-five years. My college roommate Shannon Mette and her daughter Jordan encouraged me to share my story publicly and helped me navigate the world of social media. Lisa Korn, Ronit Sherwin and Ayumi Kwade-Niwa, who were part of my daily college life, continue to be present today from afar. Lori Hanson taught me that appearances on the outside are not what is really happening on the inside, and that stepping on the grass is more than okay. And Alina Gerlovin-Spaulding, who was my rock in Florida, will always hold a special place in my heart. Jeff and Mikki and the other Bloomington crew, who provided strength and support for Jeff and myself, continue to be part of this journey.

I've been guided by the wisdom and kindness of several rabbis and educators—Rabbi Harold Berman, Rabbi Alan Cohen, Alan Edelman and Rabbi David Glickman—who nurtured my understanding of faith and healing. Todd Schemmel, PhD, a friend of ours since our boys were born, contributed his professional perspective to this manuscript, and I'm grateful for his insights and care.

To the dear friends I've made in Kansas City—Lisa Gortenburg, Lynn Harris, Netta Krashin, Dana and Neal Schwartz, Celeste Schemmel, Jenny Seifert and Beth Sherry—thank you for embracing my family and me, for quietly showing up with meals, check-ins, and unwavering presence, even when things got hard.

A special thank you to Jane Martin, who helped me begin this book. For six months, we met weekly, and Jane helped me bring my memories to life. That time together set the foundation for everything that followed. To my nephew Gabe—thank you for the honesty and insight you bring, not just as family, but as a friend who offers me real perspective and support. And my nephew Ben, who has shown me that if I love myself first, the love of others will follow.

Sometimes, thank you isn't enough. So, to Aaron Feldman—my ghostwriter, but more importantly, my life-long friend—thank you for stepping into this project with your whole heart. You've helped bring this story to life, capturing my voice, honoring the voices of others, and shaping a book that I hope can offer support and connection to anyone touched by mental illness. You've believed in me, and this story, from the beginning—and you gave it your all. I'm also thankful to those you brought into this process—including Rick Dahl, a gifted producer, writer, and friend who graciously served as copyeditor of this book.

There are countless others who have impacted my journey—from childhood through today. Many of my family members, whom I am not able to name individually, continue to support me and my family, and the mental health world. I've worked alongside brilliant professionals in the nonprofit world, teenagers who challenged me in the best ways, and lifelong friends from BBYO and Camp Ramah who taught me about faith, loyalty, and community. I've been uplifted by generous funders who trusted me to serve Jewish Kansas City with passion and integrity. And I remain in awe of the staff and board at First Call, who fight daily to erase the stigma around substance abuse and mental illness.

To the many therapists, psychologists, psychiatrists, educators, trainers, and the compassionate team at Onsite in Tennessee—thank you for your belief in healing and your commitment to care. You've helped me find myself again.

Finally, to Shirley, whenever I said "It's raining outside," you'd remind me, "Karen, it's always sunny outside." Thank you for your impact and perspective that stays with me.

RESOURCES

I WANT TO end with a few resources. Not because I believe any one of them holds the magic answer—but because I believe in second chances. In safe spaces. In trying again.

If you're in crisis:

- **988 Suicide & Crisis Lifeline:**
  Call or text 988 (24/7, free & confidential)

- **Crisis Text Line:**
  Text HOME to 741741

- **The Trevor Project:**
  1-866-488-7386 or thetrevorproject.org

For long-term support:

- **Mental Health America:**
  Screening tools, community resources; mhanational.org

- **National Alliance on Mental Illness (NAMI):**
  Peer groups, education, advocacy; nami.org

- **Open Path Collective:**
  Affordable therapy directory; openpathcollective.org

- **Onsite:**
  Cumberland Furnace, TN; (800) 341-7432,
  https://experienceonsite.com

For families and caregivers:

- **Child Mind Institute:**
  Support for raising kids with mental health conditions; childmind.org

- **Al-Anon:**
  Help for families of those struggling with addiction and mental illness; al-anon.org

Books I recommend:

- *Will I Ever Be Enough? Healing the Daughters of Narcissistic Mothers* by Karyl McBride, PhD

- *Children of the Aging Self-Absorbed: A Guide to Coping with Difficult, Narcissistic Parents & Grandparents* by Nina W. Brown, EdD, LPC

- *Getting Past Your Past: Taking Control of Your Life with Self-Help Techniques from EMDR Therapy* by Francine Shapiro, PhD

- *The ACOA Trauma Syndrome: The Impact of Childhood Pain on Adult Relationships* by Tian Dayton, PhD

ABOUT THE AUTHOR

KAREN B. GERSON is a writer, advocate, and survivor who uses her lived experience with mental illness to break stigma and inspire understanding. Her debut memoir, *I Should Not Be Here*, explores the ripple effects of OCD, PTSD, and depression—not only on those who live with them, but on the families and communities who love and support them. Through honesty, vulnerability, and hope, Karen's work reminds readers that survival itself is an act of courage.

A lifelong educator and community leader, Karen has dedicated over twenty years to program development and youth engagement within the Jewish community. She has also worked extensively with First Call, an organization that reduces the impact of substance use disorder where she's honored to serve on the Board of Directors.

Born and raised in Columbus, Ohio, Karen earned her Bachelor of Science in K-8 Education from The Ohio State University and her Executive Master of Public Administration from the University of Missouri-Kansas City. She has lived in Leawood, Kansas, for more than 25 years with her husband, Jeffry, their two sons, Gilli and Eitan, their dog Skeye, and Stuart the "big" bunny.

When she's not writing, Karen can be found watching her boys play soccer, cheering for Sporting Kansas City, practicing yoga, traveling to her favorite places like Israel and Costa Rica, and celebrating life's moments with friends and family.

Please visit my webpage to learn about resources and/or get in touch with me.

karenbgerson.com